Christian and Divorced

What the Bible REALLY Says About
Divorce & Remarriage

Eitan Bar

Contents

Part III

Divorce According to Rationality

Preface

I don't think the Bible allows divorce and remarriage ever while the spouse is living. That's my radical, crazy, conservative, narrow, hard-nosed, very needed view in our divorce-happy culture.[1]

(Pastor John Piper, a Baptist pastor)

Without exception, divorce is a product of sin, and God hates it. He never commands it, endorses it or blesses it.[2]

(John MacArthur, a Calvinist pastor)

The Bible doesn't seem to regard persistent, unrepentant physical abuse as a valid ground for divorce...the decision to leave a persistent abusive partner shouldn't be arrived at lightly...If church leaders establish that physical abuse is recurring in a marriage, they should recommend only a temporary separation.[3]

(The Gospel Coalition, a Calvinistic magazine)

I encountered such quotes early in my journey as a Jewish follower of Jesus. Coming from a Jewish background, I was initially puzzled by the stark difference in views on divorce and remarriage between Judaism and Christian fundamentalism, which includes the Messianic movement I was very active in. It took me years to realize where the bone of contention lay.

Upon completing this book, you'll be equipped with the intellectual tools needed to both understand and refute common misconceptions about the Bible's stance on divorce and remarriage. This includes the ability to critically evaluate and challenge the classic perspective of Christian fundamentalism, as illustrated by the above quotes. Given the technical nature of some sections, I recommend reading this short book thoroughly without skimming or skipping.

---

1. https://www.desiringgod.org/interviews/does-the-bible-allow-for-divo rce-in-the-case-of-adultery

2. https://www.focusonthefamily.com/marriage/the-dilemma-of-divorce

3. TGC is considered the "hub" of modern-day Calvinism.

Divorce

The English word "divorce" originates from the Latin "divortium,"[1] meaning 'separation,' 'division,' or a 'parting of ways.' For instance, in classical Latin literature, you might find "divortium" used to describe a geographical separation, such as a fork in a road or a river, or metaphorically to describe a divergence of opinions or a separation of allies. This term is akin to "divort" or "divortere," where "di" signifies *apart*, and "vertere" translates to *turning in different directions*. The term entered the French lexicon in the late 14th century and appeared in Middle English around the same time. Like most other words, "divorce" has significantly changed its meaning over time. Today, in modern times, the word "divorce" is commonly understood as a formal declaration that legally ends a marriage.

To understand the biblical concept of divorce, one must explore its non-Western historical context, especially during biblical times. In that era, divorce was a complex process involving social, legal, and religious aspects, adapted to a society where polygamy was prevalent, and women were considered property with minimal rights.

This short book aims to unravel these complexities, offering a nuanced view far removed from contemporary Western fundamental interpretations. It explores the intricate process of divorce, its cultural and legal implications, and its varied impacts. By the conclusion of this book, readers will have a deeper, biblical, more informed perspective on divorce, appreciating both its positive and negative aspects within the broader historical and biblical framework. However, given the vast scope of the topic, I will only provide a bird's eye view of divorce.

---

1. "Middle English divorse, from Anglo-French, from Latin divortium, from divertere, divortere to divert." (Merriam-Webster Dictionary)

Introduction

A marriage is one of life's most profound commitments, embodying not just a personal union but also a societal cornerstone. This partnership offers a deep emotional and spiritual connection, providing a safe space for vulnerability, growth, and the joys of companionship. Open communication, trust, and mutual respect are paramount in a healthy marriage. Partners support each other's goals, share compassion, and collaboratively resolve conflicts while maintaining their individual identities. Such a relationship, marked by a balance of giving and receiving, ensures both partners feel valued and heard.

On an emotional and spiritual level, marriage enhances life satisfaction and mental health, offering a sense of security, purpose, and meaning. It allows individuals to explore and deepen their spirituality, finding strength in shared values and beliefs. Children, in turn, benefit from the stable, loving environment of a healthy marriage. They are more likely to develop strong emotional and social skills, perform better academically, and have lower risks of engaging in risky behaviors. The example set by their parents' relationship teaches them respect, love, compromise, and what healthy relationships look like.

A healthy marriage is a life-enriching partnership that upholds and cherishes the values of mutual understanding and support, making it a vital and cherished institution in both personal and communal spheres.

But no marriage is without its challenges. Staying together through the hardships of marriage can be an avenue for profound growth, both individually and as a couple, allowing the relationship to serve as a crucible for personal transformation. When a couple chooses to stick it out even when things get tough, they create a powerful shared narrative that speaks to resilience, commitment, and the depths of their emotional and spiritual investment in one another. This steadfastness can also be immensely reassuring for children, who see a model for navigating life's complexities and uncertainties in their parents.

A long-lasting marriage offers the opportunity to grow old together, to share the big and small moments that accumulate over a lifetime, and to build a lasting legacy that can provide a sense of purpose and continuity that honors God and sets an example for others to follow. The marital relationship also becomes a source of support in life's later stages, when health might falter, and external friendships may fade. The shared history and mutual investment in each other's well-being become invaluable assets, reinforcing the idea that a lasting marriage can be one of life's most rewarding endeavors despite its challenges.

Overcoming trials together strengthens the marital bond, creating a form of intimacy that is deeper and more multifaceted than the infatuation that characterizes the honeymoon phase. Moreover, weathering storms as a united front cultivates a sense of mutual respect and reliance that can be exceptionally fulfilling. On a practical level, maintaining a marriage avoids the emotional and financial strains of divorce, such as splitting assets and renegotiating familial roles, which can introduce additional stressors and complications.

Furthermore, marriages are crucial to social stability and community strength as married couples contribute positively to societal welfare. The stability and economic advantages of married house-holds have a ripple effect, promoting overall community well-being. In essence, marriage, founded on love, respect, and commitment, is a personal blessing and a societal asset. It nourishes the mind and soul, provides a nurturing environment for children, and contributes to community stability. Better communities mean a better world.

This is God's will for all marriages.

When 'Happily Even After' Isn't the Case

What I described above encapsulates, without a doubt, God's ideal vision for all marriages. However, life doesn't always unfold according to our plans and hopes. Building on this, I want to express a deep concern about the significant misunderstandings surrounding the topic of divorce within the realms of Christian fundamentalism.[1] This misunderstanding can have far-reaching repercussions that stem partly from inaccurate Bible translations and a failure to appreciate the nuanced Hebrew and Jewish context in which pivotal figures like Moses, Jesus, and Paul delivered their teachings.

Far too often, Jesus's teachings are interpreted in isolation, devoid of their historical and cultural setting, especially the social norms pertaining to the role and status of women in Judaism at that time. In antiquity, women were not commonly perceived as independent entities; they were often regarded as property, either "owned" by their fathers or husbands. Furthermore, it was not uncommon for men to have multiple wives, further complicating the dynamics of marital relationships. On top of that, women could not formally initiate divorce; only men could, which often led to wives leaving their houses to find another man while still married, resulting in adultery.

The prevailing logic within some fundamentalist circles is rooted in a rigid interpretation of biblical texts that seems to permit divorce only in the cases of sexual infidelity. Such an interpretation disturbingly omits consideration for other—often more severe—forms of mistreatment, such as physical and emotional abuse, financial exploitation, being married to a psychopath-narcissist, etc.

This oversight had tragic consequences for Dasha, a friend of mine. Despite wishing to divorce her abusive husband, her messianic church elders pressured her otherwise, compelling her to stay in an abusive marriage that eventually led to her tragic death—she was murdered by her Christian husband using a hammer. That happened in 2023, just a few minutes from where I live. I have known that family for twenty years.

Several months before her death, a couple in her church who had decided to peacefully divorce was asked to stand in front of the entire congregation. The elders announced that they were divorcing and, as a result, would no longer be allowed to participate in the congregational communion. From that point on, they would be considered merely visitors. Imagine Dasha sitting in the crowd, witnessing her church's degrading and humiliating treatment of someone who had just gone through a divorce. Surely, this further pressured her to stick with her abusive husband, fearing the same mistreatment from her church.

In the wake of Dasha's tragic murder, I engaged in heartfelt conversations with many of her close friends. They revealed that she had longed for a divorce, a will that met with intense pressure from the church to remain in her marriage because "God hates divorce." Moved by this revelation, I penned an extensive Facebook post. This action opened a floodgate of private messages from numerous women, each sharing her own harrowing tales. They spoke of pastoral interventions that shattered their family lives, of being compelled to endure abusive relationships, and more. These profound interactions inspired me to author this brief book.

What exacerbates the fundamentalist illogicality even more is the additional stipulation that not only should individuals like Dasha not divorce, but should they do so, they would also be barred from remarrying. This raises a troubling ethical question: in such an interpretation, why is the victim the one being penalized?

For several millennia, legalistic religious interpretations of divorce and remarriage have inflicted deep wounds. These range from young individuals coerced into marriages against their will to abused spouses trapped in harmful relationships, with some tragically ending up killed by their violent partners. The flawed theology surrounding divorce, damaging many lives, often also shattered the paths to healing, restoration, freedom, and the opportunity to start over that God has laid out in the scriptures (e.g., Exodus 21:11).

This book is intended as a sanctuary for those enduring loveless, unstable marriages, whether suffering from emotional starvation or physical abuse and seeking a way out. It's for those who feel isolated in their pain and fear they will be living in adultery if they enter a new marriage. May a proper, healthy interpretation of the Scriptures shield us against legalistic misinterpretations of Scripture. The book also honors children stigmatized by their parent's divorce, often wrongly seen as a sin rather than a remedy for sin. It's for partners judged for leaving destructive relationships. To all of you, this book is dedicated.

***

In this short book, I will explore the key Bible verses related to divorce and remarriage, highlighting the frequently ignored and misunderstood Jewish context, translation nuances, and logical inconsistencies in the fundamental teachings about divorce. Additionally, I will examine why divorce sometimes is, both biblically and rationally, essential for a healthy society and the welfare of individuals.

Please note that throughout this work, I will be using a variety of Bible translations. Also, keep in mind that this is a micro-book, not a 500-page volume, so the focus has been on covering the essential aspects.

For better flow, I decided to divide the book into three main sections:

Part I: *Divorce & Remarriage in the Old Testament*
Part II: *Divorce & Remarriage in the New Testament*
Part III: *Divorce & Remarriage According to Rationality*

---

1. Judaism views divorce and remarriage quite differently from Christianity. While Judaism can sometimes be legalistic, it typically allows divorce much more freely than most Christian denominations.

Part I

Divorce & Remarriage in the Old Testament

Critical Terms

"Divorce"

A modern English word without a direct single-word equivalent in the Biblical Hebrew language describing the end of a marriage.

"Put Away"

The physical removal of someone. In the context of divorce, this would be of the spouse, usually the wife, and usually in a public way. Some English translations of the Bible incorrectly translate the term *"put away"* as *"divorce."*

Hebrew: "SHALACH" or "GARASH" | **Greek:** "apoluó"

"Bill of Divorcement"

A formal written certificate confirming the legal end of a marriage contract ("GET") releasing a woman from the ownership of her husband. This includes the amount agreed upon in advance, as written in the Ketubah, due to the woman in the event of a divorce. This is the closest term to modern English "divorce."

Hebrew: "SEFER KERITUT" | **Greek:** "apostasion"

"Agunah"

A Jewish term for a wife being put away by her husband without a legal bill of divorce. This issue has sparked significant disputes in Judaism for thousands of years while remaining largely unknown to most Christians. It was a contentious topic that led to debates between Jesus and religious Jews.

Chapter 1

Cultural Backdrop

Divorce in Ancient Babylon

The earliest recorded law on divorce dates back to 1760 B.C., during the reign of King Hammurabi of Babylon. The Code of Hammurabi, an ancient Babylonian law code, is a crucial historical document that provides insight into the societal norms of the time when the Torah (Law of Moses) was written, particularly concerning the covenant of marriage and divorce. This code, which predates the biblical laws given to Israel by Moses, was established by the Babylonian king and reflects the cultural and legal standards of the early Old Testament period.

Believed to have inscribed 282 laws on stone tablets, Hammurabi included regulations for divorce.[1] In that era, a man could divorce his wife by simply declaring she was no longer his wife, which could necessitate the payment of a fine and the return of the wife's dowry.

Divorce in the Code of Hammurabi was allowed under certain conditions, often favoring the party deemed "innocent." Men could verbally terminate the covenant of marriage for various reasons, leaving the woman with nothing and no formal documentation of the separation. The process was skewed towards men, who could easily challenge the divorce or refuse to provide the agreed dowry.

> In event a man's legal wife shall depart from him after having been guilty of extravagance, and before her departure she is brought to court by her husband and the husband solicits a divorce, which is granted, she shall be permitted to depart and the husband shall not be compelled to compensate her. In event the husband does not desire to be divorced and desires to take another wife, the one deemed guilty of extravagance shall be compelled to remain in the house of her husband as a servant.
>
> Code of Hammurabi, law 141.

Conversely, if a wife sought a divorce, she had to present a formal complaint and was seldom granted a separation. If she was able to divorce, she was likely to be considered damaged goods. However, it was hazardous for a wife to file for divorce. In that society, women needed men for protection.

The laws of Hammurabi significantly influenced the context in which the Law of Moses was given. In fact, the Law of Moses was established to contrast Hammurabi's laws, which explains the frequent similarities between the two laws.

Understanding this context helps set the backdrop against which the laws of Moses were given. It is against these prevailing norms that the corrective measures of the God of Israel were introduced, adjusting and implementing changes without necessarily repeating every aspect of the contemporary law. Moses's teachings on marriage and divorce were very limited because they were framed in response to these already established practices, tailored to the understanding of his contemporaries.

Covenants

In Christian biblical studies, there is often an overlooked complexity in understanding the concept of a covenant, one of which the average Bible student may not fully be aware of. Specifically, it's essential to distinguish between *conditional* and *unconditional* covenants. Broadly speaking, there are two types of covenants presented in the Scriptures: 1. Conditional covenants (fault); 2. Unconditional covenants (faultless).

Conditional Covenants: These agreements set forth specific conditions to which the parties must adhere. These covenants are breakable. For example, if one party fails to uphold their end of the agreement, the other party is entitled to terminate the covenant. Marital covenants fall into this category, as they are agreements where both individuals commit to certain terms and understandings. This concept of conditional contracts was widely recognized and practiced in the Ancient Near East, with both the Code of Hammurabi and the Mosaic Law recognizing the principle of conditional stipulations in agreements (e.g., Deuteronomy 28-30).

Unconditional Covenants: These agreements are not dependent on the recipient's actions or failures. They are promises made unilaterally, where one party commits to fulfilling the covenant regardless of the other party's behavior. A good example of unconditional covenants are God's covenants in Genesis 9 (Noah) and in Genesis 15 (Abraham).[2]

To provide a clearer example of a conditional/fault covenant in everyday terms, imagine a parent who promises their child ice cream if the child manages to sit still and remain quietl during a meeting. The understanding is that if the child successfully meets the condition of remaining still, the reward of ice cream will follow. This agreement is contingent upon the child's behavior. If, however, the child is restless, moves around, talks, and does not sit still, then the condition has not been met, and the parent is not obliged to provide the ice cream. This scenario is a simple yet effective illustration of a *conditional covenant*: fulfilling the promise hinges on the child's adherence to the agreed-upon behavior.

This understanding is crucial when examining the context of biblical marriage and divorce. Just as ancient covenants had stipulations that could render them void in the case of misconduct, the marital covenant, too, was seen as conditional. If one party violated the sacred terms of the marriage, the wronged individual had the right to seek the dissolution of the covenant, aligning with the broader legal and cultural practices of the time. Thus, the concept of conditional covenants provides a framework for understanding the biblical allowance for divorce as a rightful response to the breach of marital vows. In the Law of Moses, violations included, for example, instances when the husband reduced or failed to provide enough food, clothing, and marital rights to his wife (Exodus 21:9-11). In such cases, the wife had the right to seek divorce. The Law of Moses prioritized the individual's well-being over the marital institution's sanctity.

Marriage Covenant

In biblical times, many men had multiple wives, and often, marriages were not about love or personal choice but were arranged by parents as part of financial or power agreements between families.[3] Often, the man could choose, but the woman had no say. With this context, it's crucial to understand that the marriage laws of the biblical period were designed primarily to protect the legal status of the woman—who was considered property—and to secure her legal rights. This was because she was seen as the more vulnerable and disadvantaged of the two sexes. The Torah laws do not focus much on the theological aspects of marriage but are more concerned with the technical aspect, primarily aiming at protecting the weaker vessel.

From a biblical perspective, a marital covenant is inherently <u>conditional</u>, unlike some modern Christian interpretations, which often view it as a bond beyond reproach. In the Ancient Near East, marriage contracts were distinctly recognized as conditional contracts, crucial for the welfare and prosperity of individuals and societies. A marriage is a deliberate pact between two parties, where each agrees to specific terms and understandings. They vow to honor these terms and publicly declare them.

In Jewish tradition, this contract is known as a ***Ketubah***, which literally translates to "written thing" in Hebrew. A "Ketubah" is a legal document accompanying the wedding ceremony, outlining the husband's obligations to his wife, primarily concerning financial commitments in the event of divorce or widowhood. Giving the ketubah to the bride during the wedding ceremony is still customary today. The Jewish Ketubah is a conditional agreement that notably includes a provision for dissolution—divorce. The earliest Ketubah found was in Egypt, written on papyrus in Aramaic, and dates from 440 B.C.

This further proves that marriage in Judaism was seen as a <u>conditional</u> covenant.

This ancient understanding starkly contrasts with some fundamentalist Christian views disregarding the Law's conditional nature. Various Christian ideologies consider marriage vows absolute, expecting both parties to remain committed regardless of almost any breach. Conversely, modern Western laws align more closely with biblical principles, acknowledging the right to dissolve a marriage when the contractual terms or understandings are violated. These violations can be manifold, ranging from infidelity, abuse, and emotional abandonment to breach of trust, change of critical life values, severe lack of chemistry, and irreconcilable differences, each constituting a failure to uphold the sacred terms initially agreed upon within the marriage covenant. As in biblical times, only the couple has the exclusive right to decide whether to seek a divorce. It is the couple's choice, and they will benefit and/or suffer the consequences, whatever they are. God does not stand in their way or "punish" them for their choice.

In the West, about two-thirds of divorces are initiated by women. A study in the UK estimates the main proximate causes of divorce, based on surveys of matrimonial lawyers, to be:

Adultery – 27%

Family strains (e.g., from the inlaws) – 18%

Domestic violence – 17%

Midlife crisis – 13%

Addictions, e.g. alcoholism and gambling – 6%

Workaholism – 6%

Other factors – 13%

In all these instances, the dissolution of marriage is not the ultimate desire of God, who intends for couples to live in harmony, love, and mutual respect, forgiving and extending grace to one another. However, divorce represents a necessary concession crafted to protect the well-being of those involved—now and in the past. By permitting the dissolution of marriage, God acknowledges that the sacredness of human well-being takes precedence over the sacredness of an institution.

Consider the divine marriage between God and Israel at Mt. Sinai, where Israel pledged to adhere to God's commandments (Exodus 19:3-8). In return, God promised Israel the heritage, kingdom, honor, and protection He previously promised Abraham (Genesis 12:1-3). When Israel reneged on this sacred agreement, spurning numerous chances for redemption, her 'Husband' lawfully enacted a divorce, formally documented, and sent her away (Jeremiah 3:8; Hosea 2:2). If, as some argue, "God hates divorce," then why would He divorce Israel?

This scriptural precedent shows that even in a divine context, the covenant of marriage, which is conditional, carries stipulations and the possibility of dissolution should those stipulations be disregarded, emphasizing that marital vows are not to be taken lightly. Still, neither are they to be seen as irrevocable in the face of the risk to the individuals' well-being.

The allowance of divorce is a critical aspect of any functioning society, embodying the acknowledgment that individuals must have the right to set boundaries, experience freedom, and pursue personal well-being. This principle is not only a matter of civil liberty but also aligns with the biblical precedent set for the people of Israel, where divorce was permitted to safeguard individual dignity and welfare. Such a provision acknowledges that individuals are not possessions; rather they possess inherent worth and autonomy as humans created in the image of God with free will.

Marriages, while sacred, should not be held in higher regard than the mental and physical well-being of the individuals within them.

The Sabbath was made for man, not man for the Sabbath (Mark 2:27). Likewise, marriage serves man and woman; it is not their master. To enforce the inviolability of marriage at the expense of human welfare would be to objectify individuals, stripping them of their God-given freedom to thrive and live without harm. In this light, the permission of divorce serves as a divine concession to human imperfection and societal necessity, ensuring that personal sanctity is preserved above the marital bond.

---

1. Code of Hammurabi, laws 127-194.

2. It is my personal conviction that salvation in the New Testament is also unconditional.

3. Matchmaking is still widespread in modern Orthodox Judaism, but it is more flexible today than it was in the past.

Chapter 2

Moses on Divorce

B ecoming "one flesh" is the ideal of any marriage, a model established with the first couple in Genesis 2:24. However, it faltered
after the fall when Adam blamed Eve for his eating of the forbidden
fruit.[1] This breach of trust in their union marked a turning point.
Since then, 'one flesh' has represented an ultimate standard akin to
residing with God in the Garden of Eden. Since we've left Eden,
perfection remains unreachable in our fallen world. The hardness of
the human heart, often seen in couples turning against each other, is
the backdrop as to why divorce is a legitimate reality in the Scriptures.
The Bible, primarily through Moses, sought only to set boundaries
and regulations, not to dictate whether anyone should or shouldn't
divorce. The choice to divorce or stay together was in the hands of the
couple alone, not in the control of the elders of Israel.

The primary biblical source for the laws of divorce is found in
Deuteronomy 24:

The passage takes the practice of divorce for granted and is attempting to regulate a particular variation of it. Divorce was a reality, in Israel and elsewhere. How common it was is unclear, but enough passages in the Old Testament refer to it that we must conclude it was not uncommon.[2]

Since the reasons for divorce vary, the Law spoke in general terms:

> When a man takes a wife and marries her, and it happens that she finds **no favor in his eyes because he has found some indecency** in her...
>
> (Deuteronomy 24:1-2; first half)

According to the Law, a woman who commits adultery is sentenced to death by stoning (Leviticus 20:10-12; Deuteronomy 22:22-24). Therefore, in contrast to what some teach, *"some indecency"* cannot refer to adultery:

> Adultery, however, cannot be supposed here *(some indecency)* because that was punishable with death.[3]

While I believe Moses intentionally spoke in general terms, throughout history, Jewish and Christian theologians and commentators have attempted to explain the terms *"no favor"* and *"some indecency"* (erwaṯ dāḇār[4]), and many interpretations exist. For instance:

Something indecent (erwaṭ dāḇār) may have been a technical legal expression; the precise meaning is no longer clear. The same expression used in 23:14, where it suggests something impure, though the words do not seem to have normal connotations. In this context, the words may indicate some physical deficiency in the woman, though this meaning is uncertain. A physical deficiency such as the inability to bear children may be implied.[5]

Regardless of the husband's reason for divorcing his wife, he was required to follow the Law. Unlike the Pagans, he couldn't simply dismiss her without proper procedure. Jewish scholar Professor Corinadeli explains:

The foundations of the act of divorce in the Torah are threefold: **(a)** the writing of a bill of divorcement by the husband; **(b)** its delivery to the woman ('and he shall put it in her hand'); **(c)** the sending away of the woman from the husband's house ('and he shall send her out of his house'), meaning a practical separation between the spouses.[6]

Unlike modern English, the Hebrew Bible lacks a single word to encapsulate the entirety of the divorce process. Instead, there are three distinct stages/terms. The key verses that discuss the procedure for divorce in Deuteronomy 24 are verses 1-2, which state that if a married man wishes to end his marriage, he may do so by following the Law's procedure:

1. He writes a *bill/certificate of divorce*.

2. He hands it to his wife.

3. He *puts away* his wife, usually publicly sending her from his house.

Afterward, she is free to marry again:

> ...*he writes her* **a certificate of divorce** *and* **puts it in her hand** *and* **sends her out** of his house, and she leaves his house and **becomes the wife of another man.**
>
> (Deuteronomy 24:1-2; second half)

Clearly, the Law allows for divorce and remarriage. The Law's approach to divorce is pragmatic, acknowledging the reality of failed marriages while setting a high bar for the sanctity and permanence of the marital relationship. It is important to note that the Law does not encourage nor discourage divorce but merely provides regulations for its conduct.

Since people can decide to marry, it's only reasonable that they could also choose to divorce, although that is not the ideal outcome God desires. Couples who stay together for decades provide valuable lessons for society; marriage should not be taken lightly, and divorce should not be the easy way out. However, if a marriage becomes detrimental to your body, spirit, or soul, exiting that marriage could, sometimes, be a necessary protective measure.

The written 'certificate of divorce' served as formal evidence for the divorced woman but also prevented her former spouse from making future claims against her. This method surpassed the Code of Hammurabi, where the absence of witnesses to a husband's verbal dismissal left the ex-wife without dissolution proof. The God of Israel's commanded written decree was an additional measure to protect divorced women from malicious ex-husbands. Still, this compassionate act was occasionally exploited.

Once the three steps to dissolve the marriage are finalized, if she then marries another man and the second marriage ends either through divorce or the husband's death, the first husband cannot remarry her (verses 3-4). This law was meant to protect the woman from being threatened or treated poorly, like a piece of property that could be discarded and taken back at the husband's whim.

If Deuteronomy focuses on the "how," **Exodus 21:10-11** exemplifies some of the "why." These verses speak of the woman's rights, especially in the context of those given into marriage by her father as part of a financial agreement (verse 7), likely in disregard to her will. If her husband later takes another wife/concubine, a common practice in those times, he must not diminish her food, clothing, or marital rights. If he does not provide her with her basic needs, she is free to divorce without any fine. This passage is one of the earliest indications in the Law not only of divine permission to divorce but also of God's attempt to protect women living in a hyper-chauvinistic society. Here, fundamentalists must confront a challenging question: Why would God seek to protect a woman from an abuser by allowing her to divorce if He believed she should remain with him?

Exodus 21 provides only illustrative cases. There are countless other possible scenarios and reasons for the 'whys,' making it unrealistic to expect the Bible to serve as a manual for when divorce is permissible. In the Jewish view, the decision is left to the couple, not anyone else. The Law simply comes to anchor the divorce process in law to protect the individuals involved.

The process outlined in the Law is further developed in the Jewish Talmud, where the rabbis discuss various grounds for divorce, the steps to divorce, the rights of the involved parties, and the specifics of the "*GET*" (GET is the rabbinic term for the *bill of divorce*). The GET is the most crucial component of a Jewish divorce; without it, the woman is not free to remarry, and any subsequent relationships are considered adulterous. For example, if a husband refuses to give his wife, who left him, a GET, thereby preventing her from moving on with her life, yet she proceeds to marry another man, both she and her new partner would be living in an adulterous relationship. This was not uncommon.

Regrettably, some Jewish men—then and now—exploit this technicality by physically separating from their wives ("*put away*") without granting them the GET (bill of divorce), preventing them from moving on and finding new love. This tactic allows the husbands to "punish" their wives while also avoiding alimony payments. In Judaism, a woman trapped in such a predicament is called an *Agunah* ("chained woman").

According to Jewish law, for a marriage between Jewish partners to be legally dissolved, the husband must willingly give a divorce document (GET) to the wife, who in return must accept it. The Rabbinical court is authorized to impose a range of sanctions on a man who refuses to grant a GET. Sanctions can also be imposed on a woman who refuses to accept a GET from her husband, but this requires approval from the president of the Great Rabbinical Court.

Consider this scenario: An Israelite husband, acting cruelly towards his wife, drives her into the arms of another man. In a punitive response, he withholds the bill of divorce, trapping her in a state of Agunah (anchored or chained) and preventing her from moving on legally. Overwhelmed by bitterness and frustration, she defies her marital bonds and chooses to marry her new love regardless. In this complex tapestry of actions and reactions, who is primarily responsible for the ensuing adultery? Such dilemmas have been central to Jewish theological discourse for more than three millennia, engaging even figures like Jesus, the Pharisees, and the teachers of the Law. Christianity often disregards this complex interaction between personal autonomy, religious law, and moral ethics.

Divorces initiated by God

The Pentateuch contains narratives that illuminate the nature of divorce from God's perspective. One example is the story of God instructing Abraham to *send away* Hagar (Genesis 21:14),[7] which can be seen as an early form of divorce. This incident happened before Moses established a legal framework, during a period when Abraham was subject to Mesopotamian law, where a legal document was not necessary for divorce.

Later, in the prophetic writings of the Hebrew Bible, marriage and divorce are potent metaphors to describe the Law-based covenantal relationship between God and Israel. The prophets often employ the imagery of marriage to symbolize the intimate covenant between God and His nation. The imagery of God divorcing Israel is used to represent the severing of this relationship due to Israel's spiritual infidelity.

For instance, the prophet Hosea's life is a dramatic enactment of this metaphor. God commands Hosea to marry Gomer, a woman of promiscuity, to symbolize Israel's unfaithfulness. The tumultuous marriage of Hosea and Gomer reflects the betrayal of Israel through idolatry and moral failure, and their reconciliation mirrors God's unwavering willingness to forgive and restore (or "remarry") the broken relationship.

While the primary message of the book of Hosea is about God's enduring love for Israel despite her unfaithfulness, the literal narrative focuses on Hosea's marriage to Gomer, a woman who was unfaithful to him. Hosea's willingness to take Gomer back even after her betrayal can be seen as an example of unconditional love and divine grace. However, this example could also be examined to highlight the deep emotional and spiritual complexities that can arise in a marriage and how divorce may sometimes become necessary.

Moreover, the concept of God divorcing Israel is repeated in passages such as Jeremiah 3:8, where God declares that He had given Israel a certificate of divorce and sent her away: "*I gave faithless Israel her certificate of divorce and sent her away.*" This metaphorical divorce signifies God's judgment upon Israel for her spiritual unfaithfulness. However, the prophetic narrative does not end with divorce; it later speaks of restoration and renewal. The prophets, including Hosea and Isaiah, foretell a future where the relationship between God and Israel is restored, akin to a renewal of marriage vows, perhaps to highlight God's enduring love and commitment to His people despite their waywardness. Regardless, the fact that God did divorce Israel remains.

To summarize this section, the Law recognizes the right to divorce and establishes a framework to ensure that divorce is handled with justice, protecting the rights of the individuals while upholding the sanctity of marriage. In the Hebrew Scriptures, divorce was not a rare occurrence and was even, if only metaphorically, employed by God Himself.

Understanding the legal language and laws of the Ancient Near East is crucial when examining biblical terms related to marriage and divorce. Likewise, to fully grasp Jesus' teachings, it is essential to recognize that they are rooted in the foundational writings of Moses. Understanding Moses is critical to comprehending the consistent message that both he and Jesus conveyed. However, ignoring Moses will lead to flawed conclusions and unfounded beliefs, as we often see today.

Bearing this context in mind, let's explore one of the most critical nuances of divorce in the Hebrew Scriptures—the often overlooked distinction, particularly by Christians, between "putting away" and issuing a "bill of divorce."

***

'Put away' vs. 'Bill of divorce'

Recognize the significance of the biblical language for proper interpretation...accustom yourself to the notion that there is a linguistic and cultural distance that separates us from the biblical text. While this distance should not be exaggerated, beware of reading into the Bible ideas that can be supported only from the English translation...Do place priority on the attested and contemporary usage of words...writers depend on the way language is actually used in their time.[8]

A careful interpretation of Scripture demonstrates a consistent message from beginning to end. Crucial for our discussion, the Old and New Testaments use two primary terms to describe marital actions regarding divorce; both can be found in Deuteronomy 24:1-2:

'BILL OF DIVORCEMENT' | 'PUT AWAY'

As we discussed earlier, "divorce" is a modern English term that describes a situation where both conditions, issuing *a 'bill of divorce,'* and *'putting away'* have been met.

Bill/Certificate of divorcement = a formal divorce paper ("GET") releasing a woman from the ownership of her husband. This includes the amount agreed upon in advance, as written in the Ketubah, due to the woman in the event of a divorce.

Send/Put Away = the physical removal of someone. In the context of divorce, this would be of the spouse, usually the wife, and usually in a public way.

In the Bible, 'divorce' refers not to an action but to a document. On the other hand, 'putting away' was an action, specifically the act of physical separation.

However, some translations, like the NIV, mistakenly use the English word "divorce" to interchangeably translate both terms throughout the Bible. This has caused considerable confusion and, by doing so, has completely changed the theology of divorce. As some of these translations use *'divorce'* instead of *'put away,'* Christians often mistakenly read *'put away'* as *'divorce.'* However, *Put away* does <u>not</u> equate to the modern concept of *divorce*. This problem also exists in one of the Hebrew New Testament translations.[9]

'Bill of Divorcement' (or 'Certificate of Divorce')

Judaism uses the word *GET*, while the Hebrew Bible uses a combination of two Hebrew words, *"Sefer Kritut, "*for the English term *"certificate of divorce." Sefer* means a bill, paper, book, scroll, or certificate. *Kritut* means "cutting."[10] In Hebrew, Sefer Kritut literally translates as *"Book of Cutting."*

David Brewer, a Jewish studies researcher from Cambridge University, explains why the certificate of divorce was crucial for any woman being put away:

> It was a great advantage for a woman to have a certificate stating that her former husband relinquished any right to her, and allowed for her to marry any man. Without it, she would have great difficulty finding a

second husband if she was abandoned or dismissed from her home by her first husband.[11]

The term "*Certificate of divorce*" (or "*Sefer Kritut*" in Hebrew) only describes the first part of the process: the legal part of the divorce process. This includes detailing the amount agreed upon in advance, as written in the Ketubah, due to the woman in the event of a divorce.

In other words, "*divorce*" or "*divorcement*" translated in your English Bible encompassed only the legal certificate—*Sefer Kritut*—in Biblical Hebrew. The issue is that the term "put away" is often mistranslated, translated also as "divorce" in English translations, causing much confusion to the non-Hebrew reader.

While the term "*put away*" (or "*send away*") is seldom related to the term "*bill of divorce*," the term "*bill of divorce*" always appears in conjunction with the term "*put away*" (e.g., Deuteronomy 24:1,3; Isaiah 50:1; Jeremiah 3:8), a testament that two should go hand in hand as part of a divorce process:

> This is what the LORD says: "Where is your mother's **certificate of divorce** with which I **sent her away**? Or to which of my creditors did I sell you? Because of your sins you were sold; because of your transgressions your mother was sent away."
>
> (Isaiah 50:1)

And I saw that for all the adulteries of faithless Israel, I had **sent her away** and given her a **writ of divorce**,

yet her treacherous sister Judah did not fear; but she
went and was a harlot also. Because of the lightness
of her harlotry, she polluted the land and committed
adultery with stones and trees...

(Jeremiah 3:8-9)

In the context of marriage, while wives were often *put away*, they
were not always granted a bill of divorce. However, if they were granted the bill, they would always be put/sent away. In cases where wives
were put away without the bill of divorce, they would become "*Agunah.*"

Remember, marriages were typically transactional. They usually
involved some form of dowry. If a man only slept with a woman, he
had to pay a dowry, regardless of whether they married or not (Exodus
22:16-17). Often, the husband had to make a payment, either to the
bride's father, as a dowry in money, assets, estate, or through work if
he couldn't afford it, as seen in Genesis 29 and Genesis 31:14-15. In
other cases, the wife's family paid the husband.

In addition, and as you probably know, polygamy was a common
practice during the biblical era. Polygamy served, among other things,
as a means for men of higher social status to maintain marital relations
with women from lower economic and social classes. In such cases,
the man's wife from the higher status was considered his primary wife,
while the woman from the lower status was a 'concubine,' usually a
wife with much less privileges.

For example, Leah, Rachel, Bilhah, and Zilpah, the four wives of
Jacob, were all daughters of Laban the Aramean. Rachel and Leah
were daughters of Laban's principal wife. At the same time, Bilhah
and Zilpah were born to another woman, a maidservant from the
slave class, with whom he had a concubinary relationship. When Leah

married Jacob (without his knowledge), her father gave them Zilpah as a maidservant. When Rachel married, they received Bilhah as a maidservant.

Back then, husbands could—and often did—*put away* their wives without granting them a *bill of divorce*, thereby saving themselves from losing money, assets, maidservants, or other valuables.

'Put Away' (or 'Send Away')

In the Hebrew Bible, "*put away*" (or "*sent away*") derives from the Hebrew words "SHALACH" (to send away) and "GARASH" (to drive away or to expel), with the latter being more negative. For example, both words are used in Genesis 3:23-24 when God expelled Adam and Eve from the Garden of Eden. Likewise, *Put/send away* is also used in many other non-marital verses. For example: *"And Isaac **sent away** [SHALACH] Jacob: and he went to Padan-aram unto Laban, son of Bethuel the Syrian, the brother of Rebekah, Jacob's and Esau's mother."* (Genesis 28:5)

In the context of marriage, "*put away*" was used to describe a man who physically removed his wife from his home for one reason or another. There were reasons other than divorce for why a spouse might "*put away*" and not live with the other, such as a contagious disease like leprosy or being compelled by their family for various reasons.

In the context of divorce, this action initially did not involve providing a bill or certificate of divorce until the Law of Moses mandated it. The introduction of writing and giving a certificate of divorce represented a new requirement—not found in earlier laws—to which the men of Israel struggled to adjust.

For this reason, the Law forbids Jewish men—priests included—from taking as wives women who were only put away. For example:

> They shall not take a wife that is a whore, or profane;
> neither shall they take a woman *put away* from her
> husband...
>
> (Leviticus 21:7; KJV)

Leviticus forbids marrying a woman *put away* by whom? By her husband. But if *'put away'* merely meant she was divorced—she no longer has a husband.

To conclude, *"put away"* (or *"send away"*)—SHALACH (or GARASH) in Hebrew—meant only the physical removal or expulsion (of the wife, in most cases, in the context of marriage). At the same time, the *"bill of divorcement"* was the legal document formally and officially terminating the marriage. It is crucial to differentiate between the two; otherwise, we might arrive at strange, very unbiblical conclusions.

One such example is Malachi 2:16.

Malachi 2:16

> "For I hate SHALACH," says the LORD the God of
> Israel.
>
> (Malachi 2:16)

While some English translations wrongly use the word *"divorce."* (*"For I hate divorce."*), some, like the KJV, used *"putting away"* in translating Malachi 2:16: *"For the Lord, the God of Israel, saith that he hateth putting away..."*

What is taking place in chapter 2 of Malachi?

First, recall that through Ezra, God directed the Levites to *put away* their foreign wives (even if they had shared children; Ezra 10:3). This is a "catch-22" for the fundamentalist interpretation because if "put away" meant "divorce," then here God requires the Levites to divorce, something He allegedly hates.[12]

Anyways, the Levites would *put away* their first wives as well as take additional ones, usually foreign ones. On the one hand, these first wives faced degradation; on the other, they were merely put away without receiving a legal bill of divorce so they could receive back their dowery and move on to find new husbands. It was this act of putting away (without the proper legal formal procedure instructed earlier in the Law) that God hates![13]

Israel's Law required men to provide a written certificate of divorce rather than merely put their wives away (aka, turning them Agunah). In Malachi 2, the men of Israel failed to do so, which led to God's rebuke. The reason God was upset becomes clear with context:

> *Because you have not kept My ways, but have shown* ***partiality in the instruction***.

> (Malachi 2:9)

When men put away their wives without giving them a proper divorce document, it is to show partiality in the instruction. In other words, these men only partially followed the—more convenient for them—biblical prescribed procedure for divorce as ascribed by Israel's Law, thereby denying their wives liberty and the freedom to remarry.

It would be bizarre to suggest that God, who divorced Israel, commanded Abraham and the Levites to put away their wives and integrated guidelines for divorce in His Law, would suddenly claim He hates and forbids divorce. On the other hand, it makes much more sense that He hates putting away without fully following the process prescribed in His Law of giving the necessary document.

In fact, no one until recently ever associated Malachi 2:16 with divorce, as Christian fundamentalism does today. Historically, interpretations vary, but even the most conservative commentators do not interpret it as an attack on divorce. A few examples below:

> No instance can be quoted of these verses being understood in earlier times as an attack on divorce. The LXX and the Tg. take v 16 not as a prohibition against divorce but as a permission to divorce one's wife. And (5) interpreting this passage as an attack on apostasy to an alien cult is in agreement with the rest of the book of Malachi.[14]
>
> Smith, R. L.

> Judean men were marrying women from other ethnic groups in the region who worshiped pagan gods...T he prophet's overriding concern was not marriage, as such, but the effect of an unwise mixed marriage on a man's relationship to the Lord.[15]
>
> Ted Cabal

Septuagint, "If thou hate her and dismiss her," etc.;
Vulgate, "If thou hate her, put her away," which seems
to encourage divorce.[16]

Donald Spence Jones

---

1. Remember, when God forbade Adam from eating from the Tree of Knowledge, Eve hadn't been created yet.

2. Gerald Gerbrandt, Deuteronomy: Believers Church Bible Commentary, 2015.

3. Spence-Jones, H. D. M. (Ed.). (1909). Deuteronomy (p. 381). London; New York: Funk & Wagnalls Company.

4. The term is mentioned elsewhere in the Bible, but sometimes not even in reference to sexuality.

5. Craigie, P. C. (1976). The Book of Deuteronomy (p. 305). Grand Rapids, MI: Wm. B. Eerdmans Publishing Co

6. The Personal Status of the Karaites by Michel Corinaldi, Dr. Jur. 1984.

7. The text uses the same word, SHALACH, as in Deuteronomy 24:1.

8. Kaiser, Introduction to Biblical Hermeneutics: The Search for Meaning, 2007., p. 63-64

9. The <u>modern</u> Hebrew word used today by Israelis (which is also used in one of the modern Hebrew translations of the New Testament, which is based on the NIV) to describe the entire 3-step divorce process is *GIRUSHIN*. This can be confusing for modern Hebrew speakers because the word is derived from the biblical word GARASH. However, Judaism and the Hebrew Bible use different terms.

10. From the Hebrew word *KARATH*, meaning 'to cut off.'

11. D. Brewer, "Deuteronomy 24:1–4 and the Origin of the Jewish Divorce Certificate"

12. Remember John MacArthur's declaration: "Without exception, divorce is a product of sin, and God hates it. He never commands it, endorses it, or blesses it."

13. The word "hate" is also often misunderstood, as it is sometimes confused with the modern and emotional concept of "hate." You can explore this topic further in my micro-book *"Lost in Translation: 15 Hebrew Words to Transform Your Christian Faith."*

14. Smith, R. L. (1998). Micah–Malachi (Vol. 32, p. 323). Dallas: Word, Incorporated.

15. Cabal, T., Brand, C. O., Clendenen, E. R., Copan, P., Moreland, J. P., & Powell, D. (2007). The Apologetics Study Bible: Real Questions, Straight Answers, Stronger Faith (p. 1396). Nashville, TN: Holman Bible Publishers.

16. Spence-Jones, H. D. M. (Ed.). (1909). Malachi (p. 23). London; New York: Funk & Wagnalls Company.

Chapter 3

Agunah ("Chained Wife")

I n biblical times (as well as modern Orthodox Judaism), women could not formally initiate divorce; only men could. In this ancient patriarchal society, men often married several women, but a woman could not marry more than one husband. If a woman desired to leave her marriage, the man was required to provide her with a certificate of divorce, along with any associated financial settlement. This, however, wasn't that easy, as men would often *put away* their wives without granting them a divorce certificate. In this situation, a woman is defined as Agunah:

> An agunah (chained woman) is a woman whose marriage has in fact ended or been suspended but who legally remains a married woman (bound to a husband who no longer lives with her) and thus is unable to remarry.[1]
>
> Ronald L. Eisenberg

Jewish Bible professor Amnon Bazak notes that the non-issuance of a bill of divorcement for a wife sent away by her husband will result in the woman being considered an Agunah.[2] Professor Grossman echoes similar sentiments.[3] The same is being made clear in the Talmud.[4]

Simply put, an Agunah is the name given to a woman whose husband has put away without granting her a legal divorce certificate; she is practically divorced (separated) but not legally. The argument in Judaism was: Is it lawful to marry an Agunah (woman separated from her husband) or not? This debate is still very much alive and continues to this day. To whet your appetite, here is a short excerpt from an article in a well-known Israeli newspaper:

> Is Agunah Tamar Epstein's Remarriage Legal Without Orthodox Divorce? Epstein, who has conducted a high-profile, years-long campaign to force her recalcitrant ex-husband to grant her a religious bill of divorce, appeared recently to have found a way around her dilemma. Tamar Epstein, the prominent "chained woman" whose right to remarry under traditional Jewish law was long stymied, may have finally found two Orthodox rabbis willing to help her wed again.[5]

The term "Agunah" originates from the Hebrew word for anchor (moor), visually depicting a chained married woman unable to move on.

The plight of the Agunah, or chained wife, is a critical moral challenge in Jewish law. Not following the 3-step procedure prescribed in the Law has led to situations where women are unable to remarry since their husbands refuse to grant a GET/divorce certificate, effectively leaving them in a legal state of limbo.

The issue of Agunah has been intensely explored in Judaism in both rabbinic and scholarly discussions, revealing the situation's complexity.[6] These wives were legally chained to their husbands but not living with them, or in other words, women whom their husbands had *put away* without granting them a *bill of divorce*. They were practically—but not legally— divorced. The most typical case involves a husband who has disappeared or put/sent away his wife without the necessary certificate, leaving these women unable to remarry within the faith.

Many Israelite women who were *'put away'* by their husbands without a bill of divorce and became Agunah managed to find shelter with another man, which sometimes was a life-saving solution for them. However, since their previous marriages had not legally and formally ended, they were not considered divorced according to the Law and, therefore, were regarded as adulteresses if they married another man. Without the *bill of divorce*, they were not legally divorced but still married to their first husbands.

This, sometimes, was a way for husbands to get revenge or punish their wives/handmaids/concubines. A classic example can be found in 2 Samuel 20:3:

> Then David came to his house in Jerusalem, and the king took the ten women, the concubines whom he had left behind to take care of the house, and put them in custody and provided them with food, but did not have relations with them. So they were locked up until the day of their death, living as widows.
>
> 2 Samuel 20:3, NASB

Today, in the Western Christian world, the status of a woman as a chained deserted wife ('Agunah') does not exist because modern law generally prevents it. However, this phenomenon always existed in Judaism, even today.

Agunah in New Testament times

The Hebrew term *"put away"* (SHALACH) is represented in the New Testament by the Greek word *"**apoluō**"* / *"**apolysē**."*

For example, Mark 15:11 says, "Pilate *release* Barabbas." The Greek word translated into the English *"release"* is *"apolysē,"* meaning to put/send away, indicating a <u>physical</u> release (Pilate obviously did not divorce Barabbas.)

However, in marriage-related verses, some modern English translations have chosen to use the word *'divorce'* instead of *'put away.'* I believe this error, at least partly, stems from Christianity's unfamiliarity with the concept of Agunah.

Again, the New Testament's *"apoluō"* / *"apolysē,"* much like the Old Testament's *"put away,"* indicates only a <u>physical separation</u>, not the legal dissolution of marriage. Therefore, "divorce" would be the wrong word choice.

To better illustrate, see the comparison below between the modern English translation, the NIV, and the older King James version, using Mark 10:11, where the word *apolysē* is used:

> Anyone who **divorces** his wife and marries another woman commits adultery.
>
> NIV

> Whosoever shall **put away** his wife, and marry anoth-
> er, committeth adultery.
>
> KJV

According to the NIV, remarriages are viewed as adultery. However, according to the KJV, committing adultery is when a man marries
another woman while still married to his wife, whom he had only
physically put away—an Agunah.

I am positive you can tell which translation makes more sense.

If in Mark 10:11 Jesus did speak of divorce, we would see the
Greek word *"apostasion"* being used. "Apostasion" means divorce in
its legal sense and is the Greek parallel to the Hebrew *"certificate/bill
of divorce."* The word *'apostasion'* combines *"apo"* (away from) and
"stasis" ('state,' 'standing,' 'established by law'), implying the formal
end of a marriage contract through a written document of divorce,
also known as a *certificate/bill of divorce*.

Only the combination of both *'apoluo'* (*put away*) and *'apostasion'*
(*bill of divorce*) constitutes a "divorce" as required by the Law. Remember, Deuteronomy 24:1-4 states that if a man marries a woman
and then finds something objectionable about her, he may (1) write
her a bill of divorce, (2) hand it to her, and (3) put her away. Only then
is she no longer "bound" (either married or betrothed) but "loosed"
(released from marriage through either the death of a spouse or legal
divorce.) Remember also that Jesus and His disciples were Jews who
meditated on the Law of Moses day and night (Joshua 1:8; Psalm 1:2).

The early church fathers, many of whom harbored antisemitic views, distanced themselves from Jewish practices and beliefs. This trend persisted among the traditional churches and the Reformers (namely Luther and Calvin, both of whom were extremely antisemitic[7]). Overlooking the Jewish context of Yeshua's teachings, as often happens in Christianity, inevitably results in misguided and incorrect interpretations.[8]

If a man sends away his wife without a bill of divorce and marries another woman while still legally married, he commits adultery. Similarly, a woman whose husband has put away cannot marry another man unless she has the proper divorce documents. Marrying a woman in such a situation—Agunah—is unlawful.

Choosing the correct translation is vital. Some translations claim that God views a legally documented divorce as merely a separation and, therefore, considers any remarriage as adultery. This stance conflicts with earlier divine directives on divorce and remarriage and fails to hold up logically, even within the argument that adultery is the sole justification for divorce.

Let's conclude: The Law's instructions are clear: the act of sending away ('*Put away*'; '*SHALACH*' in Hebrew, '*apoluó*' in Greek) must accompany the giving of a written certificate of divorce ('*SEFER KRITUT*' in Hebrew, '*apostasion*' in Greek). Otherwise, without a formal writ, the separated woman—Agunah—remains legally *bound* and ineligible to remarry.

Suppose a husband failed to provide a bill of divorce. In that case, he not only failed to free her for potential support from a future husband but also shared responsibility for any resulting adultery, his or hers.

Testing the hypothesis

Now, let's compare the Luke 16:18 translation in the ESV with that of the KJV:

> Everyone who **divorces** his wife and marries another commits adultery, and he who marries a woman **divorced from her husband** commits adultery.
>
> ESV

> Whosoever **putteth away** his wife, and marrieth another, committeth adultery: and whosoever marrieth her that is **put away from her husband** committeth adultery.
>
> KJV

Notice that the ESV chose *"divorce"* rather than *"put away."* Additionally, the ESV (and other translations) states, *"he who marries a woman divorced from her husband."* This translation seems illogical because if a woman is divorced, who is her husband? She has no husband if she's divorced. Remember, Jesus was speaking to Law-observing Jews. These words can only make sense if her husband had put her away while they were still legally married—Agunah. That's also why marrying such an Agunah woman would be considered adultery—she's still married to another man!

Why would a husband want to keep his wife Agunah?

What is the purpose of a husband sending away his wife without issuing the legal divorce certificate? Consider a scenario where a wife brings her own money into the marriage, and her husband puts her away without providing a legal bill of divorce. In such a case—keeping her as an Agunah—he wouldn't be legally obligated to return her money since they are not legally divorced. As a result, he would continue to control and profit from her dowry.

While the man was prohibited from depleting the original value of her dowry, he could benefit from the returns on its investment. So, from a financial standpoint, it was worth withholding the dowry (or Ketubah settlement), depriving the wife of the financial support she was due until she could remarry:

> Until the husband has returned his wife's dowry and paid her the fine, or until she has accepted it, the husband remained liable for supporting her, even if they were no longer living together. Some (ex-)husbands, then as now, tried to avoid supporting their (ex-) wives.[9]

This is why men would legally keep their wives on paper but practically put them away. Keeping them bound as Agunah was more cost-effective. Therefore, the Law aims to protect these women by requiring their husbands to provide a bill of divorce if they no longer wish to be with them. This allows the women to move on and find refuge with a new partner.

Divorce laws were meant to protect the financial aspect of the marriage as well, emphasizing the importance of providing the bill of divorce that was linked to the monetary settlement:

> The certificate was vital for the woman, especially if the document relinquished the husband's rights to her and her dowry and authorized her to return to her family of origin or to marry another man.[10]

The Agunah dilemma was—and still is—a significant conundrum in Judaism:

> Unless some workable solution is accepted, the agunah is faced with three terrible choices. She can resign herself to her desperate fate, embark on an arduous and often unsuccessful search to find a halakhic authority willing and able to find some technicality to release her from an untenable marriage, or be forced to abandon the observant Jewish community to attain personal fulfillment in a new marriage.[11]

To summarize

In the hyper-patriarchal society of biblical times, men wielded power, authority, control, and possessions, while women, often viewed as property, had limited rights. During this period, it was a harsh practice for men to abandon their wives without issuing a divorce certificate. This left these women legally bound but effectively discarded, unable to remarry, and trapped in a state of limbo, like neglected possessions. The husband, no longer providing love, care, or support, barred the wife from finding another partner who might. Some of these women did remarry, but this meant both they and their new husbands were considered to be living in adultery. The introduction of the bill of divorcement in the Bible was a measure to free women from the plight of being Agunah. It was not sin but a remedy to sin:

> Such a form of divorce, gave only into the hand of the divorced wife that which would show, that she was legitimately dismissed, and so free, both generally and before other men, and over against her husband hitherto.[12]

---

1. Ronald L. Eisenberg, The JPS Guide to Jewish Traditions, 1st ed. (Philadelphia: The Jewish Publication Society, 2004), 70.

2. Amnon Bazak, Until this day: fundamental questions in Bible teaching. Pg. 457.

3. Avraham Grossman, Pious and rebellious : Jewish women in Europe in the Middle Ages. Pg 1-18.

4. Mishnah Ketubot 7:6

5. https://www.haaretz.com/jewish/2015-12-03/ty-article/agunah-tamar -epstein-to-remarry-is-it-legal/0000017f-f744-d47e-a37f-ff7c904d0000

6. For instance, Rabbi Gershon Shalom, professor of Judaism at the Hebrew University of Jerusalem, as part of an international team of special-
   ists, examined a fragment of ancient parchment dated back to the time
   of Moses that sheds light on Jewish divorce law and the plight of the
   Agunah. These scholarly investigations and historical analyses highlight
   the ongoing struggle to reconcile the challenges faced by Agunah wives
   with the principles of Jewish law, underscoring the complexity and depth
   of this issue within the Jewish legal and religious tradition. https://blo
   gs.timesofisrael.com/the-agunah-key-a-true-story-that-never-happened

7. For an in-depth exploration of antisemitism in the church, see *"Reason
   #2: What Was Done to Us in Jesus's Name —Christian antisemitism &
   Replacement Theology."* in my book, *"Why Don't Jews Believe in Jesus."*

8. For insightful tips on how to read and understand the Bible more effectively, be sure to check out my book *"Read Like a Jew: 8 Rules of Basic
   Bible Interpretation for the Christian."*

9. Johnson, J. (2002). Women's legal rights in ancient Egypt. University of
   Chicago Library Digital collections.

10. Daniel I. Block, Deuteronomy (The NIV Application Commentary),
    2012.

11. Ronald L. Eisenberg, The JPS Guide to Jewish Traditions, 1st ed.
    (Philadelphia: The Jewish Publication Society, 2004), 73.

12. Lange, J. P., Schaff, P., & Schröeder, W. J. (2008). A commentary on the
    Holy Scriptures: Deuteronomy (pp. 175–176). Bellingham, WA.

Part II

Divorce & Remarriage in the New Testament

Critical Terms

"Divorce"

A modern English word without a direct single-word equivalent in the Biblical Hebrew language describing the end of a marriage.

"Put Away"

The physical removal of someone. In the context of divorce, this would be of the spouse, usually the wife, and usually in a public way. Some English translations of the Bible incorrectly translate the term *"put away"* as *"divorce."*

Hebrew: "SHALACH" or "GARASH" | **Greek:** "apoluó"

"Bill of Divorcement"

A formal written certificate confirming the legal end of a marriage contract ("GET") releasing a woman from the ownership of her husband. This includes the amount agreed upon in advance, as written in the Ketubah, due to the woman in the event of a divorce. This is the closest term to modern English "divorce."

Hebrew: "SEFER KERITUT" | **Greek:** "apostasion"

"Agunah"

A Jewish term for a wife being put away by her husband without a legal bill of divorce. This issue has sparked significant disputes in Judaism for thousands of years while remaining largely unknown to most Christians. It was a contentious topic that led to debates between Jesus and religious Jews.

Chapter 4

Cultural Backdrop

Pre-Jesus era

T hroughout history, Judaism has frequently incorporated elements from contemporary cultures into its belief systems. A notable example is "Hellenistic Judaism," which describes blending Jewish religious traditions with aspects of Greek culture. This phenomenon was particularly prominent during the Hellenistic period, following Alexander the Great's conquests, which brought Greek culture into direct contact with various Jewish communities. This greatly affected Judaism, especially for the three hundred years between 323 B.C. and until Jesus' time.

This fusion of cultural and religious practices could explain deviations from Israel's law. In our case, the practice of Jewish men putting away their wives without providing the legally mandated documents, as required by the Mosaic Law, might be partially attributed to the influence of Greek legal and social customs. Greek society had its own unique approach to marriage and divorce, which much like the Babylonian law, was less formal and rigid compared to Israel's Law:

> A rare certainty in our knowledge is the ease with which a husband could terminate marriage. He had only to send his wife away, that is, back to her paternal family, and the marriage was at an end.[1]

Greek culture also influenced Christianity, known as the "Hellenization of Christianity." This influence significantly impacted early Christianity, shaping its theology, philosophy, language, and cultural context. For example, the New Testament was originally written in the Greek language, and many early Christian theological concepts were expressed using known Greek philosophical ideas.

Post Jesus era

As Christianity spread throughout the Hellenic world, an increasing number of church leaders were educated in Greek philosophy. The dominant philosophical traditions of the Greco-Roman world at the time were Stoicism, Platonism, and Epicureanism. The Catholic Church, based in Rome, is known to have been influenced by Greek culture and beliefs in several significant ways. For instance, the early Church Fathers, many of whom were well-versed in Greek philosophy, integrated aspects of Platonic and Aristotelian thought into Christian theology. This is evident in the work of St. Augustine, who harmonized Platonic ideas with Christian doctrines,[2] and St. Thomas Aquinas, whose synthesis of Aristotelian philosophy with Christian theology[3] shaped much of Catholic doctrine. Greek philosophy, containing many truths, isn't inherently negative, but it's important to recognize its influence on Christianity.

Divorce became a contentious issue in the Roman Empire after Catholic Christianity was declared the state religion in 380 A.D. In stark contrast to the Greek world, Judaism, and the Eastern Orthodox Church, which allowed for divorce, the Catholic Church has staunchly opposed it. This may be seen as an overreaction to the Greek permissiveness regarding marriage and divorce.

The shift can be traced back to a specific Christian, Saint Jerome (342-420). St. Jerome, a prominent Christian theologian, acknowledged as a Church Father and a saint by the Roman Catholic Church, was known to be a bit peculiar. He is best known for translating the Bible into Latin, known as the Vulgate. Jerome, who was never married, embraced a life of asceticism and celibacy. This was following a youthful dalliance with extravagant homosexual activities,[4] something that had greatly haunted him and affected his beliefs and views:

> And it makes no difference how honorable may be the cause of a man's insanity. Hence Xystus in his Sentences tells us that 'He who too ardently loves his own wife is an adulterer.' It is disgraceful to love another man's wife at all, or one's own too much. A wise man ought to love his wife with judgment, not with passion. Let a man govern his voluptuous impulses, and not rush headlong into intercourse. There is nothing blacker than to love a wife as if she were an adulteress.[5]
>
> Saint Jerome

Anyway, Jerome made a groundbreaking decision to translate the word *"mystery"* (μυστήριον) in Ephesians 5:32 as *"sacrament"* (Sacramentum) in the Latin Vulgate, which significantly influenced Christian doctrine regarding marriage.[6] Most translations render this verse as referring to the mystical union between Christ and the Church, described metaphorically in terms of marriage. However, Jerome's choice to use *"sacrament"* instead of *"mystery"* contributed to the Roman Catholic Church's doctrine of marriage as a sacrament, a holy and indissoluble union. This interpretation clearly influenced the Church's stance on divorce, thereby casting divorce in a severe, potentially unforgivable light.

Today, as well, the Catholic Church does not formally recognize divorce. In the eyes of the church, the Sacrament of Marriage is a life-long bond.[7] The Catholic Church's tradition of frowning upon divorce continued in the later branches that emerged from it, including the Reformed/Protestant Church. These branches almost exclusively forbade divorce, allowing it only in cases of adultery and only after conducting a thorough "investigation" by church elders.

With this background in mind, let's jump right into the gospels!

---

1. Louis Cohn-Haft, "Divorce in Classical Athens," Cambridge University Press: 23 February 2012.

2. Russell, Bertrand (1945). A History of Western Philosophy. Simon & Schuster.

3. Saint Thomas Aquinas, Stanford Encyclopedia of Philosophy Archive, May 23, 2014.

4. Robert Payne, The Fathers of the Western Church (1989), pg. 90–92. | See also: J.N.D. Kelly, Jerome: His Life, Writings, and Controversies (1975) pg. 21.

5. St. Jerome, Against Jovinianus, Bk 1, n. 49.

6. https://catholicexchange.com/7-ways-st-jeromes-vulgate-helped-to-sha pe-the-church/#:~:text=4,Ed

7. During the early period of the Roman-Catholic church, noblemen could circumvent this by seeking annulments—a dissolution of marriage granted by church authorities for certain valid reasons or on technical grounds. However, such annulments were a privilege typically reserved for the nobility and politically connected, not for the common people. This resulted in many couples practically separating while still legally married on paper.

Chapter 5

Jesus

Jesus wasn't a Catholic priest from Rome, a Texan Baptist preacher, an Anglican clergyman in the UK, or a Pentecostal pastor in California. He was Yeshua, a Jewish Israeli rabbi who, in His Sermon on the Mount, addressed misapplications of the Jewish Law, aka the Torah. In Matthew 5:17-19, just a few verses before His famous words concerning marital issues, Jesus asserts His commitment to the Law, rejecting any notion of nullifying it and rebuking those who disregard even the smallest of commandments. This was part of the 'Jesus vs. Pharisees' debate and Jesus's overall argument for an ethical interpretation of the Law that exceeds that of the Pharisees and teachers of the law:

> Do not think that I have come to abolish the Law or the Prophets; I have not come to abolish them but to fulfill[1] them. For truly I tell you, until heaven and earth disappear, not the smallest letter, not the least stroke of a pen, will by any means disappear from the Law until everything is accomplished. Therefore anyone who sets aside one of the least of these commands and teaches others accordingly will be called

least in the kingdom of heaven, but whoever practices
and teaches these commands will be called great in the
kingdom of heaven. For I tell you that unless **your
righteousness surpasses that of the Pharisees and
the teachers of the law**, you will certainly not enter
the kingdom of heaven.[2] (Matthew 5:17-20 NIV)

Jesus's sermon upholds various Torah commandments, including
prohibitions against murder, adultery, false witness, retribution, and
the command to love one's neighbor,[3] in much higher standards than
that of the Pharisees. In this context, <u>His teachings on divorce and
remarriage must also be seen as a clarification of the Law of Moses</u>.

Jesus reminded the Pharisees that the intent behind the Law should
be upheld in spirit and truth. His intention was not to dismiss the
practical application of the Law when offering spiritual guidance in
marital disputes. The fault lay with the husbands who misused the
Law through technicalities to mistreat their wives, who had no means
to fend for themselves. Jesus had no issue with the Law itself, which
permitted divorce. His aim was not to correct His Father's Law but
rather to challenge and rectify the Jewish traditions that misinterpret-
ed it.

During His Sermon on the Mount, Jesus did not alter the practical
enactment of any commandment. Instead, He deepened its application to spring from a place of inner purity rather than mere technical
compliance or, in the context of divorce, only partial adherence. For
instance, when discussing murder, He did not amend the Law but
extended its scope to address the heart's attitude toward anger, using
the commandment against murder as a foundation. The underlying
assumption behind the fundamentalist interpretation is that in the
Sermon on the Mount, Jesus altered the Law concerning divorce and

remarriage but not concerning any other commandment of Moses, which seems unlikely.

As we covered in the previous part, some instructions were being misapplied, with the true spirit of the Law overlooked by those who wielded its letter to sidestep the more significant justice issues, especially concerning women. Employing a "technicality" to mistreat women contradicts the Law's purpose. Contrary to some popular secular accusations, Jesus was, in fact, upholding women's rights against those who would undermine them. He did so by emphasizing their right to a legal divorce certificate when being put away by their husbands so they could love, be loved, and be taken care of again by another man.

Matthew 5:31-32

"*Anyone who marries a divorced woman commits adultery*" (Matthew 5:32b) is often cited by fundamentalists against remarriage. This interpretation suggests a blanket statement that remarriage following divorce constitutes adultery, implying that almost no divorce can ever render you free to remarry. This view interprets Jesus's words as punishment for divorced people, basically saying: *Was your first marriage a failure? You may not get a chance to start anew, regardless of whose fault it was.*

In this view, Matthew 5:32b would appear to state that remarriage after divorce is adultery and that no divorce is truly binding since divorced women can never be considered free to marry again, a view that is a complete misunderstanding and contradiction to God's words in Deuteronomy. Let's compare.

Moses, allowing remarriage:

> After she leaves his [previous husband's] house she
> becomes the wife of another man.
>
> Deuteronomy 24:2

Jesus, allegedly contradicting Moses:

> Whomever marries a divorced woman commits adul-
> tery.
>
> Matthew 5:32b, NIV

If the NIV translation and the fundamentalist view were accurate, and Jesus did indeed forbid remarriage, it would present several contradictions and issues. However, just for the sake of argument, let's test the fundamentalist hypothesis that in this verse, Jesus is teaching that divorce is only permitted in cases of adultery:

1. Under the Torah (Leviticus 20:10, Deuteronomy 22:22), the punishment for adultery was not divorce but stoning to death. If the spouse dies, there's no point in a divorce.

2. It's unfair and unreasonable that a woman who has been divorced by her husband is the one punished by being prohibited from remarrying. Say she is 16 years old, and a month after getting married, her husband decided to divorce her against her will; why should she be the one punished? What kind of vengeful and unjust God punishes a woman for her husband's decision to divorce her of his own accord? However, it does make sense that she would be considered

an adulteress if she was not *'divorced'* (NIV) but *'put away'* (ASV) without a proper certificate of divorce and then engages in relations with another man—after all, she is still legally married to her first husband!

3. It's unreasonable that a Jewish rabbi would teach Jews that although their God-given Law allows divorce and remarriage, it would be sinful for a man to marry a divorced woman. This would imply that Jesus contradicts Moses. However, considering Jesus's words just a few verses earlier, saying He did not come to abolish the Law (Matt. 5:17), the possibility of contradiction is eliminated. This leaves us with a logical inconsistency where remarriage appears to be both permitted and forbidden in the Bible. Either that or some translations, such as the NIV, are biased.[4]

4. Since most modern divorces are not due to adultery, does that mean that millions who have divorced and remarried actually live as adulterers in God's eyes? That, unless you are a Puritan fundamentalist, doesn't seem reasonable. Assuming no adultery has occurred, the original marriage of the divorced couple is allegedly still valid in God's eyes. In that situation, the individual who got remarried is in limbo, for they now allegedly commit adultery. Should they divorce so as not to continue living in the stage of adultery? Imagine millions, then and now, living in constant anxiety, unsure if God is mad at them, uncertain if their second marriage is even legit or not.

5. Since many Christians believe that Jesus previously taught that lusting in one's mind is adultery (Matthew 5:28), that

must mean Jesus allows divorce when one of the spouses simply looks at another person with lust. In this scenario, a thought is grounds for divorce, but physical abuse or neglect isn't. That also doesn't seem reasonable.

For these and other reasons, I believe the best word to use in translating Matthew 5:32 is not "divorce" but "put away." This was done in other translations, such as the American Standard Version:

> Now it was said, "WHOEVER SENDS HIS WIFE AWAY IS TO GIVE HER A CERTIFICATE OF DIVORCE"; but[5] I say unto you, that every one that **putteth away** his wife, saving for the cause of fornication, maketh her an adulteress: and whosoever shall marry her when she is **put away** committeth adultery.
>
> Matthew 5:31:32, ASV

According to the ASV translation, there is no contradiction between Moses and Jesus, who reinforces Moses' words: If you put away your wife without giving her a certificate of divorce, and she goes and marries another, they both commit adultery.

"Porneia" (Fornication/sexual immorality)

> I say unto you, that every one that putteth away his wife, saving for the cause of fornication (porneia)...

Notice that the cause cited is not 'adultery' but rather 'fornication,' sometimes translated as "sexual immorality." Both 'adultery' and 'fornication' are used in the verse, but they are distinct terms with different meanings. The Greek word for 'fornication' is 'porneia,' while the word for 'adultery' is 'moicheia.' These are not interchangeable terms. Fornication does not equal to adultery.[6]

What is Fornication?

> The word "fornication" is used in the Scriptures to mean several different things...A figurative use of the word "fornication" appears in both the OT and NT. Originating in descriptions of Israel and the church as the Lord's wife or the bride, apostasy from God and idolatry are called fornication (see, e.g., Jer 2. Rv 14:8; 17:2, 4; 18:3; 19:2).[7]
>
> Baker Encyclopedia

> This word is more frequently used in a symbolical than in its ordinary sense. It frequently means a forsaking of God or a following after idols (Isa. 1:2; Jer. 2:20; Ezek. 16; Hos. 1:2; 2:1–5; Jer. 3:8, 9).[8]
>
> Illustrated Bible Dictionary

The most frequent uses of the word "fornication" in the Bible refer to idolatry and prostitution, but the term is not limited to these contexts. Paul uses "fornication" to describe another forbidden sexual union, incest, first described in Leviticus 18:6-8. In 1 Corinthians, Paul writes:

> It is reported commonly that there is *fornication* among you, and such *fornication* as is not so much as named among the gentiles, that one should have his father's wife.
>
>   (1 Cor. 5:1 KJV)

In Hebrews 12:16, Esau is described as a "fornicator" because, in Genesis 26:34, Esau took Hittite women. In Jeremiah 3 and Ezekiel 16, we find examples of Israel committing fornication by worshiping other gods—idolatry.

While some interpret fornication concerning adultery, it might be more accurate to understand the term as referring to 'forbidden unions.' A father sleeping with his daughter like Lot did (Genesis 19:30-38) or a bother sleeping with his sister, these forbidden unions are considered fornication (Leviticus 18:9).

In other words, whether sexual or not, <u>fornication is an illegitimate/unrecognized/forbidden union in the eyes of God</u>. In the context of divorce, illegitimate marriages require no bill of divorce since these unions are not recognized or considered lawful in the first place.

Suppose Elizabeth Hoad, the woman who married her Golden Retriever in 2019, decides to divorce it. In that case, no court of law will issue her a certificate of divorce, as a union between a human and a dog isn't recognized as legitimate in the first place. Likewise, if one marries his own daughter, it is also considered fornication, and there is no need for a bill of divorce to be given as their marriage isn't recognized to begin with. This was often true in cases of Israelite men marrying gentile women. Therefore, one can *put away* one's spouse without a legal divorce certificate in cases of fornication—unions that the Law does not recognize.

In other words, Jesus was simply refining and clarifying the commands of the Law: that it is permitted to 'put away' without providing a formal writ only in the case of fornication—unrecognized unions! Requiring a legal divorce would be akin to acknowledging that the illegitimate/unrecognized/forbidden union was legitimate, which is something considered unlawful according to the Law.

apoluó

> It hath been said, whosoever shall ~~divorced~~ *put away* (apoluó) his wife, let him give her a *writing of divorcement* (apostasion). But[9] I say unto you, that whosoever shall ~~divorced~~ *put away* (apoluó) his wife, except for the cause of fornication [illegitimate/unrecognized/forbidden union], causes her to commit adultery: and whosoever shall marry her that is ~~divorced~~ *put away* (apoluó) commits adultery. (Matthew 5:31-32)

The accurate interpretation becomes clear when reading Matthew 5:31-32 with a closer examination of the Jewish context and the original Greek text.

In Matthew 5:31-32, the same Greek word '*apoluó*' appears three times. However, in English, it is sometimes translated as "divorced" and sometimes as "*put away*" when it appears in the first and second

occurrences. The third instance of *'apoluó'* is almost inclusively translated as *"divorced."* So confusing!

Remember, the English term "divorce" has historically been syn-
onymous with physical separation, but today, it holds a legal meaning
as well. In other words, the English term "divorce" nowadays means
a combination of physical separation (put away) and the issuing of
a legal divorce certificate. However, to more accurately convey the
original meaning of 'apoluó,' it is preferable to use an English term that
reflects only the physical separation: "to put away," "to send away," or
"to release."

In Matthew 5:31-32, Jesus says that only in the case of illegiti-
mate/unrecognized/forbidden union (fornication) is there no need
for an official certificate of divorce as the marriage is invalid in the
first place. Otherwise, without a formal divorce document, the act of
merely sending away one's wife can lead to adulterous circumstances
for her and any who subsequently marry her, as she is still legally
married to another man. In that case, remarriage is indeed forbidden.
However, if a woman marries her brother, for instance, her brother
should send her away without a certificate of divorce.

Let me offer a paraphrase of Jesus's argument in Matthew 5:31-32:

> The Law says, *"Whosoever sends away his wife, let him
> give her a divorce certificate."* This means that whoso-
> ever sends away his wife without a legal certificate
> of divorce, unless in the case of an illegitimate/un-
> recognized/forbidden union which would require no
> divorce bill, causes her and her new partner who took
> her in to commit adultery because she is still legally
> married.

Matthew 19:9

Matthew 19:9 says pretty much the same. But notice the difference between the popular NIV translation and the KJV:

> I tell you that anyone who *divorces* his wife, except for sexual immorality, and marries another woman commits adultery.
>
> NIV

> And I say unto you, Whosoever shall *put away* his wife, except it be for fornication, and shall marry another, committeth adultery: and whoso marrieth her which is *put away* doth commit adultery.
>
> KJV

The first notable difference is that the NIV opted for the terms *"divorce"* and *"sexual immorality"* instead of *"put away"* and *"fornication."* The second notable difference is the latter part of the verse: *"and whoso marrieth her which is put away doth commit adultery,"* which is completely missing in the NIV translation.

This second half—omitted in the NIV—only makes sense if the woman was only physically *'put away'* because, in that case, marrying her while she is still legally married would result in adultery. If she is already legally divorced, then Jesus would be contradicting Moses, something He clearly wouldn't do (Matthew 5:17).

One more thing worth noticing is the term *"another woman,"* ἀπολελυμένην (apolelymenēn) in Greek, which literally translates as *"her [that is] put away."*

The first part of Matthew 19:9 should be read this way:

> Whosoever shall *put away* his wife, except it be
> for fornication [illegitimate/unrecognized/forbidden
> union], and shall marry *her that is put away*, commit-
> teth adultery.

In short, what Jesus is saying is that you cannot marry someone who left their spouse unless they first got legally divorced. Otherwise, it would be considered adultery. The only exception is illegitimate/un-recognized/forbidden marriages.

Jesus repeats His point to His disciples in Mark 10:11-12:

> When they were in the house again, the disciples
> asked Jesus about this. He answered, "Anyone who
> puts away his wife and marries another woman com-
> mits adultery against her. And if she separates from
> her husband and marries another man, she commits
> adultery." (Mark 10:11-12)

Jesus again explains to His disciples that, in contrast with other traditions, the Law forbids you to put away your spouse and grab another. You must first formally and legally divorce them. And if a woman physically leaves her husband and goes and marries another, she commits adultery because she is still legally bound.

Understanding the Logic: Why This Interpretation Makes Sense

What happens if one spouse is abusive, engaging in behaviors like physical violence, mistreatment, starvation, hatred, humiliation, cruelty, etc. but does not commit sexual immorality? Can the abused partner leave this marriage? The answer hinges on your translation/interpretation of "apoluó": *Divorce* (as translated by the NIV) or *"put away."*

If interpreted as in the NIV, it implies that a woman could be physically and emotionally abused by her husband but still not be permitted to divorce him. However, if "put away" is the chosen translation/interpretation, it suggests that in cases of illegitimate/unrecognized/forbidden marriages, a certificate of divorce is not needed. In other scenarios, however, divorce might still be an option, but a formal divorce certificate must be issued and given.

It would be absurd to suggest that God expects a person to endure a lifetime of abuse, mistreatment, negligence, cruelty, or other forms of suffering by their spouse, permitting divorce only in cases of adultery. This absurdity is amplified when considering Jesus' earlier words just a few verses before about looking at women with lust. Consequently, modern fundamentalist pastors often equate watching porn with committing adultery. In this perspective, watching porn becomes a valid ground for divorce, while physical and emotional abuse by a spouse does not.

I am not making a straw man argument. There are many examples. For instance, Paige Patterson, president of Southwestern Baptist Theological Seminary, advised abused wives in his congregation to stay with their abusive husbands. For instance, in one of his teachings, he admitted:

> I had a woman who was in a church that I served and
> she was being subject to some abuse and I told her,
> I said "All right, I want you to do this every evening.
> Get down by your bed as you go to sleep, get down
> by the bed when you think he's just about asleep, pray
> and ask God to intervene." I said, "Get ready because
> he may get a little more violent when he discovers it."
> Sure enough, she came to church one morning with
> both eyes black.[10]

Prayer is undoubtedly wise counsel. However, pastors who force wives to endure toxic and abusive relationships do not represent the God of Jesus. Such counsel starkly contrasts the Biblical image of a caring and protective Father – a God of second chances who offers abundant grace, understanding, and compassion. Enforcing such endurance paints a harrowing picture of a callous and ruthless deity who finds pleasure in the agony and despair of his creations. This depiction is chillingly reminiscent of the capricious and cruel gods worshiped by pagans, far removed from the compassionate and loving nature of the God of Israel. It's an image that inflicts deep emotional distress, challenging the very essence of a benevolent and merciful God.

The belief that, in contrast with Moses, Jesus only permitted divorce on the grounds of adultery may lead to strange situations where one spouse might go to great lengths to push the other into committing adultery. For example, a wife might intentionally withhold sexual relations, driving her husband to seek gratification elsewhere, thereby giving her a "legitimate reason" to escape the vicious marriage she is stuck in. Or a situation where a husband could physically abuse his wife, emotionally torment her, or even end up in prison for life. Yet, his wife would not be permitted to divorce him because he did not commit adultery. According to this odd interpretation, the woman is the one who is punished, as she is bound to an abusive husband and seemingly obligated to endure "in the name of God." She is stuck, or in Jewish terms, an 'agunah,' for the rest of her life without the right to divorce her husband. This interpretation is not only absurd and illogical but also contradicts the nature of a compassionate and merciful Father, the God of second chances, who seeks the well-being of His sons and daughters.

To conclude, Jesus's reprimand was aimed at men who '*put away*' their wives merely verbally, as was permitted in the Greek culture and by the more ancient laws of Babylon, rather than providing a legal bill of divorce as God's Law prescribed. He was not chastising them for the act of divorcing, which the Law permitted, but for their failure to comply and complete the legal process. This incomplete obedience placed the guilt of adultery upon the husband as well, for the abandoned Agunah wives sought protection and ended up living in adultery. Here, Jesus had the mindset of a social activist addressing the mistreatment of women, not a lawyer altering existing laws or introducing new ones.

Jesus wasn't amending God's law but addressing Judaism's misinterpretation and misapplication of it. The Divine Creator is infallible and does not contrive laws that trap His people in toxic, unhealthy relationships but gives laws that create a way out and a new beginning. God's commandments are not for leading us into bondage but for guiding us out of it—His instructions are a means of deliverance from oppression, not forcing us to stay and suffer in it. Jesus fought legalist chauvinistic men who thought they could exploit and force their wives to stay with them against their will. Ironically, this idea is once again being promoted, only this time through some Christian fundamentalists.

---

1. Fulfill in the sense of demonstrating or teaching in full.

2. Many Christians interpret "enter the kingdom of heaven" as meaning salvation from hell. However, this reading is not contextually accurate, and it is not how the scriptures typically use the term. Read further in my book, 'The "Gospel" of Divine Abuse: Redeeming the Gospel from Gruesome Popular Preaching of an Abusive and Violent God.' Available on Amazon.

3. "Thou shalt not kill" (vs. 21-26); "Thou shalt not commit adultery" (vs. 27-32); "Thou shalt not bear false witness" (vs. 33-37); "An eye for an eye" (vs. 38-42); "Thou shalt love thy neighbor as thyself" (vs. 43-48)

4. "I am convinced that one reason for the rise of popular-level Calvinism in the United States over the past 30 years is because of the popularity of the NIV." (Jeremy Myers, PhD)

5. Some translations use "but" while others use "and."

6. In Galatians 5:19 and Mark 7:21, both the words "adultery" and "fornication" are used in the same verse as well, also as distinct terms.

7. Wesley L. Gerig, "Fornication," Baker Encyclopedia of the Bible (Grand Rapids, MI: Baker Book House, 1988), 815–816.

8. M. G. Easton, Illustrated Bible Dictionary and Treasury of Biblical History, Biography, Geography, Doctrine, and Literature (New York: Harper & Brothers, 1893), 265.

9. Some translations use "but" while others use "and."

10. https://www.star-telegram.com/latest-news/article210152234.html

Chapter 6

Jesus vs. Pharisees

Some Pharisees came to him to test [trick] him. They asked, "Is it lawful for a man to *apolysai*[1] *[put away]* his wife for any and every reason?"

(Matthew 19:3)

B y the time we reached the New Testament, the Jewish concept of what we, in modern English, call 'divorce' had significantly evolved. In Jesus's time, it was still the subject of a heated ongoing debate as nothing had been settled. Notice that Jesus wasn't asked if it's the right thing to do but if it's lawful—according to the Law. Israel's Law given on Sinai, of course. When interpreting Jesus' words here, it is crucial to do so through the lens of the Law of Moses, as that's what they were arguing over.

Jesus was not being asked if men could or couldn't divorce their wives, which the Pharisees knew well was lawful. The question was if they could *"put away"* their wives (without a letter of divorce.) This question was contentious during that time, with differing interpretations and practices among Jewish religious groups.

The Greek word *"apolysai" (put away)* was translated as "divorced" by the NIV. However, the same word is used in Matthew 1:19, where Joseph planned to secretly *send away* Mary, his soon-to-be wife. The same exact Greek word also appears in Matthew 15:32 when Jesus said, "I do not want to *send them away* hungry." Clearly, this word should not be translated as "divorced" in its modern-day sense (termination of marriage).

Some Pharisees came to him to test/trick him...

The question posed by the Pharisees in Matthew 19:3 can be perceived as a trick because they attempted to entangle Jesus in a controversial and divisive issue. It's similar to a scenario where, if you were running for the presidency and were publicly asked at an automobile conference about your favorite car brand, any answer you give could risk alienating a significant portion of your support. That is unless you find a way to avoid the question tactfully.

Recalling why men often put away their wives without giving them a divorce certificate is essential. If a husband does not provide his wife with the bill, he may gain two main advantages. Firstly, he can circumvent paying the dowry or 'Ketubah' settlement to his former spouse, intended to provide monetary assistance until she gets married again. Secondly, he can continue to handle any profits he acquired through her dowry. But there were also other reasons—shame, fear of judgment, family pressure, etc.

The Pharisees likely anticipated that Jesus would either align himself with one group, potentially offending the others, or provide an answer that might be seen as contrary to the Law of Moses, which could be used against him. That's why it was tricky.

"For any and every reason?"

Words with immense implications. In that era, there was a heated interpretive debate in Judaism, mainly between the House of Hillel and the House of Shammai, two opposing views[2] regarding the correct interpretation of Moses' commandments. The House of Hillel was known to be much more flexible and permissive. The House of Shammai, however, was stricter.

The Pharisees, who typically aligned with the House of Hillel, attempted to trick Jesus by posing a question about which tradition He supported. This was intended to create a conflict between His views and those of many Jews, regardless of His response. If Jesus sided with either the House of Shammi or the House of Hillel, he would win one side and lose the other no matter which way He goes. But Jesus, like the wise Jewish rabbi that He is, did not fall for their trick. Instead, He challenged them with a counter-question:

> "Haven't you read," he replied, "that at the beginning the Creator 'made them male and female,' and said, *'For this reason a man will leave his father and mother and be united to his wife, and the two will become one flesh'*? So they are no longer two, but one flesh."
> (Matthew 19:4-5)

Jesus answered by referencing the Book of Genesis. But why?

On marriage and divorce, the House of Hillel and the House of Shammai loved to argue, more than anything, over Moses' commandments in Deuteronomy 24 (see Matthew 19:7). Still, Jesus directs them to an earlier passage. In other words, it was as if Jesus was saying, *"You are arguing over the wrong verse. Go further back! Go to the source!"*

Jesus's point is that God's ultimate standard is not Exodus or Deuteronomy but Genesis. Genesis 2:24, to be specific. These words were said before the fall. In Genesis 2:18 we read:

> *The LORD God said, "It is not good for the man to be alone. I will make a **EZER** (helper) suitable for him."*

This verse offers two distinct interpretations. A fundamentalist perspective suggests that women were created in order to be servants:

> *The woman was created to **serve** man...The scriptures state that God created woman to **serve** man.*[3]

However, an alternative interpretation is worth considering. Notably, God refers to the woman as a "helper" instead of a "servant." This distinction prompts an important question: which party typically requires help, the weaker or the stronger? It is natural for the weaker party to seek assistance. And who should the weaker party look to for help? Not someone even less capable, but rather someone with greater strength or ability. This highlights the significance of the term "helper."

In the Old Testament, "EZER" (helper) is used to describe God as a helper to Israel, implying a role of strength and support, not subordination. Psalm 70:5 states:

"But as for me, I am poor and needy; come quickly to
me, O God. You are my **help** and my deliverer; Lord,
do not delay."

The word "help" in this verse is "EZER" in Hebrew, which is the
same as in Genesis. Clearly, God helping Israel does not imply that
God is subordinate or inferior to human beings.

It is essential to recognize that physical strength should not be
viewed as the sole determining factor in this context. While men may
generally possess greater physical strength than women, women can
excel in other areas, especially in emotional quality abilities, creating
a balanced and complementary dynamic. This is particularly evident
in many marriages, where men often seek guidance from their wives
when facing challenges. However, due to the fall and because the man
no longer trusts the woman, he will try to rule over her. This will cause
"sorrow" because she was not made to be his underling but his EZER.

With this, Jesus effectively nullified their question and skillfully
avoided any potential controversy.

Jesus then explains that Moses' commandments in Deuteronomy
represent not God's ultimate moral values but His compromises following the fall:

He saith unto them, "Moses because of the hardness of
your hearts suffered you to put away your wives: but
from the beginning it was not so." (Matthew 19:8).

The issue here is not about *how* to put away one's wife (and when
to provide her with a certificate of divorce), which is a separate topic
of debate, but rather the reasons *why*. Remember, the Law does not

attempt to teach all the reasons systematically, but different Jewish traditions do. Therefore, while the Pharisees initiated a legal debate to try to trick Jesus, He, in turn, transformed it into an ethical-philo-sophical discussion. Let's unpack it...

Jesus's counter-argument

As we covered earlier in the book, marriage, like most legal agreements, is conditional. God did not create a covenant where one party is un-justly bound to a contract breached by the other. Jesus's commentary on human hardness of heart should not be misconstrued as a critique of the divine Law (which permits divorce); rather, it's an indictment of our fallen reality. The sin isn't the act of divorce but a human condition that necessitates it; we need to be allowed divorce because we live on Earth, not in Eden—If everything and everyone were perfect, there would be no need for divorce (nor for marriage; see Matthew 22:30).

So, if we wish to debate God's ultimate standard, it is found in Genesis, prior to the fall and before the Law was given:

> **For this reason** a man will leave his father and mother and be united to his wife, and the two will become one flesh
>
> (Genesis 2:24)

Can you appreciate the wordplay here? The Pharisees asked, "*For what reason?*" and Jesus answered them with Genesis 2:24, "*For this reason...*"

In the preceding verses (Genesis 2:18-20), man could not find a *"help meet for him"* among the animals. However, he did find it in the woman because she was like him, the flesh of his flesh. Therefore, when a man leaves home to establish a new one, he does so not with animals but with another human being, a woman, who is 'flesh of his flesh.' A man cannot become one flesh (procreate) with a zebra, a crocodile, or a lioness; only with a woman can they become one flesh, creating a child. This blueprint makes Genesis 2:24 the starting point for any discussion over marriage and divorce.

> So they are no longer two but one flesh. What there-
> fore God has joined together, let not man separate.
>
> (Matthew 19:6)

**"<u>What</u> therefore God has joined together Let no man sepa-
rate."**

Note that Jesus didn't say *"who* God has joined together" but rather *"what."* What God has joined together is the institution of marriage itself. God laid down the framework and conditions for the creation of marriage—the sacred space where new life, children, can be brought forth. Initially, He designed marriage as a union where man and woman come together to form a new family unit. This was the divine blueprint, the ultimate standard set before the fall of the first couple and before the knowledge of good and evil entered their consciousness, a time back when they still *"felt no shame"* (Genesis 2:25) and before the woman was told that man *"will rule over you"* (Genesis 3:16).

Genesis 2:24 doesn't negate the fact that God—following the fall—also established guidelines for dissolving a marriage, as outlined in the Law (e.g., Deuteronomy 24 and Exodus 21). However, different sects in Judaism further developed their own traditions regarding marriage and divorce that go way and beyond <u>what</u> the Law commands, essentially traditions that separate couples not in the way God has established in His Law.

At first sight, it might look as if Jesus contradicted what God commanded earlier through Moses. Was Jesus overriding the Father's instructions? Only if we interpret these words as if speaking of specific couples—a common mistake. Many commentators and theologians pointed out that in these verses, Jesus was not referring to Adam and Eve nor other couples; instead, He was discussing the principle of the institution of marriage itself, the blueprint, an abstract:

> He is here speaking in the abstract, not specially of Adam and Eve.
>
> (Pulpit Commentary)

> Not the individuals, but the unity which God cemented.
>
> (Vincent's Word Studies)

> What = The unity, not "those" (the persons).
>
> (E.W. Bullingers)

"...let no man separate."

I believe *'let no man separate'* is best interpreted as *'let no man add rules to what God has already established concerning divorce.'*

For example, suppose God established the foundations for marriage and the guidelines for divorce. In that case, humans should not impose additional rules contradicting God's directives for separation as some other traditions did.

This is relevant for today as well. For instance, contrary to some traditions, couples shouldn't need their elders' approval for divorce, as this is a private matter. Unlike in some Christian denominations, the Law of Moses entrusted the divorce decision to the married individuals, not religious leaders. No one but the couple really knows the full picture and the nuances of the situation, and while others may offer counseling, it is, at the end of the day, the couple's decision. Besides, concerns about gossip and family conflicts were prevalent even then. Leaked information could damage reputations, as people tend to take sides and judge. This impacts the children, who are already distressed by the divorce. Like today, courts exist to oversee and safeguard the legal process, but the ultimate decision rests with the couple, not with any spiritual leader. An external intervention, such as pastors who feel they have the right to intrude without the couple's asking them to, can be seen as creating rules that override God's established guidelines for divorce.

This was the issue Jesus addressed when critiquing the Jewish traditions, some of which permitted husbands to expel their wives from their homes in a manner not sanctioned by God but by man, namely, without providing a bill of divorce.

Gratefully, God has established conditions for ending a marriage that go beyond the grounds of sexual infidelity, as some believe today. For example, and as mentioned earlier, a woman had the right to divorce her husband if he withholds food, clothing, or marital relations from her (Exodus 21:10-11). If this was true for the daughters of Israel living under the Law, even more so for Christians today living under grace.

God commanded Abraham to comply with Sarah's request to send Hagar away when she became troublesome, and Abraham obeyed. Ezra (10:3) instructed the Levites to divorce their wives, even if they had children together. This indicates that divorce is permissible by God, but it must be executed in accordance with God's directives, not man's. Therefore, no person has the authority to enact new laws or disregard old ones concerning divorce. If God—not man—established the institution of marriage, it is also God—not man—who dictates its termination.

---

1. The same word is used in Matthew 1:19 when Joseph planned to secretly *send away* Mary and also in Matthew 15:32 when Jesus said, " I do not want to *send them away* hungry."

2. This, to some degree, can be likened to the Catholic vs. Protestant debate, however, mostly non-violent.

3. Ivory Simion, "The War Between Men and Women", Xlibris, 2009. Pg 20. Bold emphasize by me.

Chapter 7

Paul on Remarriage

The Apostle Paul's teachings on marriage, divorce, and remarriage, particularly in 1 Corinthians 7:10-11, have been the subject of much interpretive debate within Christianity. Some contend that Paul strictly opposed divorce and remarriage, aligning with the fundamentalist view of marital indissolubility. However, a thorough examination of Paul's words, especially when understood within the context of his Jewish background and the socio-religious milieu of the Corinthian church, suggests that Paul's stance was more nuanced and, in fact, affirms the possibility of remarriage.

Because of the present crisis (1 Corinthians 7:26)

Paul's epistle to the Corinthians addresses specific concerns raised by the community. The early Christians in Corinth were navigating the complexities of their faith in a predominantly pagan society. The *"present distress"* or *"present crisis"* refers to the heavy persecution

Christians faced, which included familial and societal ostracization, exile, and execution.[1]

Many followers of pagan religions believed that failure to appease and revere their gods properly would result in calamities. Bart Ehrman, a Christian apologist, has noted that by the late second century, there was a common perception that Christians were responsible for all disasters brought upon humanity by the gods.[2]

> They think the Christians the cause of every public disaster, of every affliction with which the people are visited. If the Tiber rises as high as the city walls, if the Nile does not send its waters up over the fields, if the heavens give no rain, if there is an earthquake, if there is famine or pestilence, straightway the cry is, "Away with the Christians to the lions!"[3]

The Roman pagans offered Christians an out by making them publicly offer sacrifices, which most refused. Punishment for refusing included arrest, imprisonment, torture, and executions.[4]

In light of this, Paul's counsel on marriage and celibacy is pragmatic, aimed at minimizing the tribulations of his fellow Christians during that specific time.

As a learned Jewish rabbi, Paul was well-versed in the Torah, which, as we saw, permits divorce. The Torah also prohibits remarrying a former spouse after they have been married to another in the interim, indicating that a legitimate change in marital status is indeed possible through divorce. This understanding is key when considering Paul's perspective on remarriage.

Because of the present crisis, I think that it is good for a man to remain as he is. Are you pledged [bound] to a woman? Do not seek to be released. Are you free [loosed] from such a commitment? Do not look for a wife. But if you do marry, you have not sinned; and if a virgin marries, she has not sinned. But those who marry will face many troubles in this life, and I want to spare you this. (1 Corinthians 7:26-28)

If we choose to ignore the context (*"present crisis"*), we end up with the conclusion that Paul exclusively recommends staying single. But in 1 Corinthians 7:26-28, Paul's instruction is clear: whether you, a Corinthian, are married or not, in time of great distress, it's advised not to make significant life-altering changes. If you are, for example, about to get married (remember that in ancient times, marriage infers a family with little children), it is not a sin to do so, but you *"will face many troubles,"* which Paul *"wants to spare you this."* It can be quite challenging to hide from lions or run from an angry mob when you have babies.

1 Corinthians 7:10-11

Paul's use of the terms *"bound"* (or *pledged*) and *"loosed"* (or *free*) reflects legal marital status within the context of Jewish and Roman law. To be "bound" is to be legally married, while to be "loosed" is to be legally separated from the marriage bond, either by the death of a spouse or divorce.

....Let not the wife *depart* [chōristhēnai] from her husband; But and if she *depart* [chōristhē], let her remain *agamos*, or let her be reconciled to her husband; and let not the husband put away [aphiemi] his wife.

1 Corinthians 7:10-11 KJV

The Greek word chōristhēnai/chōristhē, translated as "depart," means a physical separation, not a legal divorce.

agamos = **unmarried or separated?**

The word *agamos* (ἄγαμος) is a confusing one in Greek because it is the negative or opposite form of the word *gamos* (γάμος). If "*gamos*" means "a wedding feast" or "wedding celebration,"[5] symbolizing a happily married couple, then "*agamos*" (*a*=negative) is the opposite; when the couple does not live happily together but in strife and separation. While some translations wrongly used the term "*unmarried woman*," others used "*separated wife*," which makes much more sense when considering Paul's instructions, "*or let her be reconciled to her husband*," because if she is unmarried, then who is "her husband"?

The NAB, for example, translated: "*and if she does **separate**, she must either **remain single** or become reconciled to her husband.*" Likewise, the Weymouth translation says, "*or if she has already **left him**, let her either **remain as she is** or be reconciled to him.*"

Paul uses the same word, *agamos* (ἄγαμος), again a few verses later in verse 34:

...*an **agamos** or **virgin** is concerned about the Lord's affairs.*

In this verse, Paul speaks of two groups of women: (1) *agamos* *(ἄγαμος)* and (2) virgins. If both meant 'unmarried women,' as some translations suggest, it would be redundant for Paul's argument to distinguish between two groups of unmarried women, and there is no reason to separate them—after all, both groups are unmarried. However, there is logic in distinguishing between the two different groups if Paul, in the first group, refers to wives physically separated from their husbands (i.e., Agunah). For this reason, some translations of verse 34 used the word *"wife"* for the first group. For example, the KJV translates: *"There is difference also between a **wife** and a virgin."*

Consider the stark contrast in the translation of 1 Corinthians 7:34:

*"An **unmarried woman** or virgin" (NIV)*

*"A **wife** and a virgin" (KJV)*

The NIV falsely translated *"unmarried woman,"* while the KJV translated *"a wife."* They are the exact opposite of one another!

Clearly, a wife is not "free to serve the Lord" unless she is an Agunah, physically—but not legally—separated from her husband.

*"Let her be reconciled **to her husband**"?*

If Paul wasn't speaking about wives but about *unmarried women*, as suggested by the NIV, then divorced women have no husbands (to reconcile with). However, Agunah wives do have husbands they can reconcile with:

The reference throughout the verse is to separation
due to incompatibility of temper, etc.; not to legal
divorce.

Pulpit Commentary

Like Moses and Jesus, Paul was aware of the concept of married
women living apart from their husbands (Agunah). He taught that
for anyone to remarry, a legal certificate of divorce from their previous
spouse is necessary before entering a new marriage. Otherwise, it is
considered adultery. Or, in Paul's own words:

> "So then, if she has sexual relations with another man
> while her husband is still alive, she is called an adul-
> teress. But if her husband dies, she is released from
> that law and is not an adulteress if she marries another
> man."

(Romans 7:3)

Given these circumstances and the times of distress, Paul recommends wives in dispute with their husbands in these hectic times
to either remain alone or return to their husbands with whom they
had a disagreement and from whom they had separated. One may
assume some who attended the church in Corinth were Christian
wives who left their unbelieving pagan husbands' households and
dedicated themselves to serving in the Lord/church. Paul encourages
these women to return home so their husbands can protect them.
Context is crucial![6]

1. Benko, Stephhen (1986). Pagan Rome and the Early Christians, Indiana University Press.

2. Kenneth Scott Latourette, A History of Christianity, p. 82 Archived June 28, 2014, at the Wayback Machine.

3. Bart D. Ehrman, A Brief Introduction to the New Testament (Oxford University Press 2004 ISBN 978-0-19-536934-2), pp. 313–314

4. Benko, Stephhen (1986). Pagan Rome and the Early Christians, Indiana University Press.

5. Strong's Concordance, 1062.

6. **Context** is one of my 8 "rules" for basic Bible interpretation. Read more in my micro-book, "*Read Like a Jew: 8 Rules of Basic Bible Interpretation for the Christian.*"

Chapter 8

Conclusion

Many Christians today hold the belief that "God hates divorce," leading some to endure abusive relationships under the impression that divorce is not a viable option. This widespread interpretation, however, overlooks the subtleties of scriptural teachings. What God truly condemns is "putting away," where a man expels a woman from his home without a formal divorce, leaving her as an Agunah in a vulnerable state.

Religious interpretations that vehemently oppose divorce at all costs essentially prioritize a non-biblical tradition over the well-being of individuals. The reality is that God is more concerned about people being harmed or staying in dangerous relationships than the act of divorce itself.

If you've been advised to remain in an abusive relationship due to religious beliefs, you've been misinformed. Taking steps to protect yourself is not a failure of faith; it's employing the logic and intellect God has endowed you with. Whether it's seeking medical help, consulting professionals, or leaving a harmful relationship, God supports proactive measures to better our situations rather than adhering to human legalism and man-made religious rules. God cares about you as an individual, not merely as part of a legal or religious system.

God's ideal is for marriages not to end in divorce but rather to thrive in love, constantly seeking forgiveness and reconciliation, even in cases of sexual immorality. However, this isn't always the case, and God understands human fallibility and recognizes situations where married couples face insurmountable challenges. In these instances, God's grace extends beyond the limits of religious tradition. While divorce may lead to loneliness, rejection, judgment, heartbreak, emotional trauma, a sense of failure, loss of security, family difficulties, financial strain, and more, it can also be a lifesaving action and a gateway to a new beginning.

Christians should seek to comprehend and value God's grace, which grants those who are divorced a chance for renewal. Furthermore, we should always remember the foundational principle that "*It is not good that the man should be alone*" (Genesis 2:18), as guiding our stance on remarriage.

We must embrace and extend God's grace, particularly to those who have experienced the arduous journey of divorce. As Christians, while we uphold the sanctity of marriage, we should also recognize human imperfections and the need for compassion, love, and support for those on the path to second chances.

Part III
Divorce According to Rationality

Chapter 9

Purity Culture and Predestination

(In the Context of Marriage and Divorce)

"*Fate has terrible power. You cannot escape it by wealth or war,*"[1] wrote Sophocles, the fifth-century B.C. Greek tragedian and pagan. Sophocles also espoused the idea that gods are the generators of both good and evil.[2] The idea of 'fate' opposes the notion of free will and refers to the development of events in a person's life that are beyond their control, often considered preordained by a supernatural force.

While the concept of an individual's fate was not familiar to the children of Israel,[3] the doctrine of fate has been prevalent in many other ancient religions. In ancient Greek mythology, for instance, the concept of fate was embodied by the Fates—three goddesses who were thought to control the course of human lives. They were responsible for spinning, measuring, and cutting the "thread of life," thereby predetermining each individual's destiny. Similarly, the Romans believed in the Parcae, personifications of destiny who directed the lives of humans. The ancient Celts of the Iron Age also subscribed to the notion of fate, believing in Wyrd, a pre-Christian goddess who predetermined life events.

The belief in fate extends to other cultures and religious traditions, even influencing modern belief systems. In Islam, the concept is known as "Qadar," which posits that everything occurring in the world, including individual actions and choices, has been predetermined by God. According to Islamic teachings, God is omniscient and omnipotent, so He has predestined all events.

Unfortunately, the concept of fate has not bypassed Christianity but has permeated some theological circles, most notably within Calvinistic theology, where it is referred to as the doctrine of "Unconditional Election." According to this doctrine, God chooses, even before a person is born, whether they will go to heaven or hell. Essentially, Calvinistic predestination suggests that, at the end of the day, human beings have no real choice or free will, likening them to mere hand puppets manipulated by divine will.

Predestination and 'Purity Culture'

Purity culture, a movement predominantly found within Evangelical Fundamentalist Christian communities, promotes the idea of predestination as it applies to marriage: the belief that God has selected one's spouse in advance. This idea is frequently used to reinforce the sanctity of marriage, suggesting that if God has predestined a union, it must be eternal and inviolable.

Introducing predestination into the realm of marriage risks trapping individuals in unions with partners they may not genuinely like, compromising personal happiness and the very essence of marital harmony. For example, one might find themselves in a lifelong commitment with someone they're incompatible with, merely because they believe it was 'predestined' by God. At an Israeli Bible College where I once taught, this belief was prevalent. I recall a student, a young woman in her 20s, who was often in tears, anxious that God might direct her to marry a fellow student. This male student was pursuing her, but she genuinely did not like him.

Purity culture advocates patiently waiting for God's direction on whom to marry. This perspective gained traction in fundamental evangelical Christianity during the last century, largely due to Joshua Harris's best-selling book, "I Kissed Dating Goodbye." Written in his early twenties, the book sold over 1.2 million copies. However, in 2016, Harris publicly retracted his views and issued an apology, declaring his own teachings false.

Predestination also affects the believer's view of divorce, which is viewed not just as a breaking of vows between two individuals but as a defiance of God's divine plan. The line of reasoning follows that if God has "elected" this person to be your spouse, then opting for divorce would be tantamount to questioning God's wisdom and acting against His will.

However, there are several problems with purity culture, such as:

1. **Oversimplification**: The belief in marital predestination oversimplifies the complex tapestry of factors that make a marriage work or fail. It reduces marriage, a multifaceted relationship with its own inherent challenges, to a single variable—God's will. This negates the roles of compatibility, mutual respect, effort, and even changing circumstances in the success of a marriage.

2. **Moral Absolutism**: This viewpoint leans heavily into moral absolutism, implying that divorce is universally wrong, regardless of the situation. This doesn't take into account marriages broken by emotional or physical abuse, neglect, or other significant hardships.

3. **Psychological Harm**: This belief can induce severe psychological stress and emotional trauma, as individuals within troubled marriages might feel they are not only failing their spouse but also defying God's will. They may feel trapped, with no morally acceptable way out.

4. **Community Judgment**: A belief that makes a divorce "against God's will" inevitably leads to a culture of judgment and stigma against those who do go through a divorce, further isolating and traumatizing them.

5. **Enduring Unhealthy Relationships**: People may commit to or stay in harmful or even dangerous relationships far longer than they should, believing that leaving is against God's will. This was very evident in the case of my friend Dasha.

6. **Emotional and Spiritual Scarring**: Those who do opt for divorce often carry a heavy burden of guilt, shame, and a sense of spiritual failure, which can have lasting repercussions on their emotional health and future relationships.

7. **Compromised Well-Being**: The societal judgment stemming from these beliefs often extends beyond the divorced individuals to include their children and extended families, creating a ripple effect of harm and stigma.

While the idea that God has predestined spouses may offer comfort to some, it's important to recognize the limitations and potential harm of such a belief, particularly as it contributes to an anti-divorce stance. Life is complex, and ethical considerations in marriage and divorce should reflect that complexity rather than a one-size-fits-all mandate purportedly derived from divine will.

My previous statement resonates with Jewish perspectives on divorce, though at times, these views have been extended to extremes. For instance, in the Talmud (Gittin 90a), one sage suggests that a man can divorce his wife for poor cooking. Initially, this might seem chauvinistic. However, contemporary rabbis interpret this as a protective measure, allowing a woman to escape a marriage where she is unappreciated or in a toxic situation. Essentially, it provides an exit from an abusive relationship. The Talmud is filled with such debates, illustrating the nuanced and adaptable nature of Jewish views on divorce that is often lacking in Christianity.

---

1. Sophocles I: Antigone, Oedipus the King, Oedipus at Colonus.

2. I believe evil is an outcome of abusing free will, not something created by God. Isaiah 45:7 doesn't suggest otherwise. Further exploration of the topic in my book: 'The "Gospel" of Divine Abuse: Redeeming the Gospel from Gruesome Popular Preaching of an Abusive and Violent God.'

3. Free Will was always a strong motif in the Old Testament. Consider: Genesis 2:16-17; Deuteronomy 30:19; Joshua 24:15; Romans 10:9, etc.

Chapter 10

The "Is-Ought" Problem

The "is-ought problem," originally formulated by the philosopher David Hume, addresses the difficulty in moving from descriptive statements about what "is" to prescriptive or normative statements about what "ought" to be. In the context of marriage, the "ought" is often idealized as a "happily ever after"—a state of perpetual marital bliss. While this ideal serves as a noble aim, it often starkly contrasts with what "is"—the actual lived experiences of many people in marriage.

The idea that marriages should strive for a loving, mutual, strong bond is deeply rooted in many religious teachings. Christians, too, believe that God's ideal for marriage is a loving, lifelong commitment between two people, often supported by scriptural references. Life, however, is replete with changing variables—financial stress, illnesses, evolving personal goals, and, unfortunately, sometimes even forms of abuse. These variables can turn what was once a loving relationship into a toxic and harmful situation for one or both partners. The "is" often diverges from the "ought," and it's in this divergence that ethical complexities arise.

The "is-ought problem" in this scenario raises an important question: Should the idealized "ought" of lifelong marital bliss override the real-life "is" of a toxic, harmful marriage? Or, to put it in other words, what is more important to God, the marriage institution or the individuals in it?

Given that not all situations can or will align with the ideal, there must be room for ethical considerations that allow divorce as a regrettable but sometimes necessary option. To insist otherwise would be to prioritize an abstract concept over tangible human well-being.

When community members pass judgment on a divorce without understanding the complex variables that led to this point, they reinforce the gap between the "is" and the "ought," exacerbating the suffering of those involved. When a side is being picked, as often happens in religious communities, the gap between the sides getting divorced only further increases. Such judgment lacks empathy and steps beyond the boundaries of privacy and what should be considered a communal domain. The decision to get divorced should only be a topic of discussion between the couple and those they decide to invite in.

While God desires "happily ever after" for all marriages, the ethical responsibility of a community should be to support the well-being of its members as they navigate the complexities of life, including the painful reality that some marriages should end for the mental health and safety of those involved. Pressuring them to do otherwise, let alone in the name of God, is a crucial error that can harm the lives of many. The "is-ought problem" serves as a reminder that judgment should not be passed on what one doesn't fully understand, especially in matters as deeply personal as marriage and divorce.

In Christian communities, where marriage is held as a sacred covenant symbolizing deep spiritual commitment, the heart-wrenching decision of divorce should ideally remain a private matter. Too often, this deeply personal issue spills into public discourse within the community, leading to unintended consequences. Religious elders and members, despite their best intentions, never really have a comprehensive understanding of the couple's private struggles and the intricate dynamics of their relationship. This lack of full insight often results in hasty judgments or biased support, overlooking the complexities at play.

The stigma attached to divorce in some faith communities further complicates the issue. Divorced individuals are often unfairly labeled as 'sinners' or 'weak believers,' leading to their social marginalization and deepening their emotional trauma. This stigma, coupled with the lack of professional psychological training among religious leaders, means that well-meaning advice often does more harm than good, especially in situations that demand nuanced psychological understanding.

Children, when part of the equation, are particularly vulnerable to the repercussions of their parents' divorce becoming a community affair. Keeping such matters private is crucial to protect them from the stress and instability of public scrutiny and gossip.

Moreover, the core principles of the Christian faith—love, forgiveness, and compassion—are often overshadowed by the public handling of divorce cases. This contradiction often manifests in judgment and exclusion rather than the understanding and support that the faith advocates. By maintaining the privacy of these sensitive issues, Christian communities can more faithfully reflect Christ's teachings, offering a more empathetic and supportive environment for those navigating the difficult divorce journey.

Chapter 11

What If It Was Your Child?

N o loving father would ever wish to see his daughter suffer in an abusive relationship, enduring physical pain or emotional torment day after day. This brings us to an unsettling but necessary question about the nature of God, who is, both in Christianity and Judaism, often portrayed as the eternal Father. This begs the question—what kind of Father is the God of Israel? Is He a protective Father who wraps His daughter in a cloak of love and fortitude, guiding her safely through the painful labyrinth of divorce? Or is He a Father who callously nudges her back into the waiting arms of her abuser?

The parallel between a loving earthly father and God as the compassionate, ultimate Father crystallizes as we ponder this. A father, in the truest sense of the word, is a guardian of well-being, a beacon of love, and a stronghold of emotional safety. Just as no earthly father would sleep peacefully knowing his daughter is imprisoned in a relationship where her worth is negated, God—revered in Scriptures as the epitome of love, justice, and mercy—would similarly rally behind His daughter's quest for liberation from a disastrous marriage. God would never condone her remaining shackled to a life filled with harm—be it physical, emotional, or spiritual. Therefore, if God personifies the zenith of paternal love and protective instinct, then advocating for the allowance of divorce in situations of abuse, neglect, or extreme unhappiness becomes not merely a social statement but a theological imperative.

By pressing for a more humane and nuanced understanding of divorce, particularly within the rigid confines of fundamental Christianity, we are essentially invoking a return to the faith's Hebrew roots, rekindling its foundational teachings on justice, compassion, and mercy. It's high time we dismantle the misunderstandings and stigmas that have long been associated with divorce. In doing so, we affirm that there are circumstances where the dissolution of a marriage is not just an unfortunate last resort but is, in fact, the most compassionate, loving, and godly course of action. To remain silent or passive in the face of suffering would be to betray not only the teachings of our faith but also the very character of God as a loving Father.

The story of Peter and Paul parting ways, as documented in the New Testament, can be seen as an instructive parallel to the concept of divorce. Both Peter and Paul were not only key figures in the early Christian church who both had a divine mandate to spread the teachings of Jesus Christ but were both sons of God. However, despite sharing this overarching aim, these brothers-in-faith found themselves in sharp disagreement over issues such as the role of Gentile converts in the church. This disagreement came to a head in Antioch, where Paul publicly rebuked Peter for withdrawing from eating with Gentiles to appease certain Jewish Christians.

The point is that both apostles recognized that their disagreement was severe enough to impede their shared mission. Their parting of ways was not a surrender to failure but a pragmatic and respectful acknowledgment that some of their differences were substantial and couldn't be reconciled. In this sense, their separation was a means to preserve the integrity of their individual callings and ministries. They chose to part ways in order to be more effective in their separate spheres, free from the discord that had characterized their relationship.

In this story, God did not intervene to stop the act, nor did He chastise Paul and Peter for their discord. This suggests that God recognizes there are times when His children reach a point in life where they can no longer grow and serve together effectively.

Likewise, divorce can sometimes be the most responsible and respectful course of action when two partners find their differences irreconcilable. It can be a boundary-setting measure, enacted not out of spite or surrender but as a deliberate act to protect the emotional and spiritual well-being of both parties and, often, the children involved. Much like Peter and Paul, who continued to be effective in their separate ministries after their parting, divorced individuals can go on to lead fulfilling lives, engage in meaningful relationships, and even co-parent effectively when the strife and emotional toll of a dysfunctional marriage no longer weighs them down.

Chapter 12

When You Are No Longer You

L ife's complexities often mirror the evolution of relationships. Picture yourself as a child with a best friend. As time passes, both of you develop distinct worldviews. Your interests diverge, and eventually, you realize you no longer enjoy the same things. Your worldviews have become so different that you no longer like this friend. Considering your shared history, you both agree to put in extra effort. You discuss your issues and even attend therapy together, hoping professional counseling will mend the rift. However, this proves futile. You've grown apart to such an extent that not only do you feel you have nothing in common, but their presence also becomes a source of distress. Are you then obligated to maintain this friendship indefinitely, or do you have the freedom to move on?

Now, consider this scenario within the context of marriage. If this person were your spouse, would you be duty-bound to remain with them forever? Depending on the situation, I would probably say.

Humans are not static beings; they are organic entities in a constant state of flux. Life lessons, personal discoveries, professional shifts, and even spiritual awakenings can send individuals down remarkably divergent paths. Marriage vows often speak of "growing together," but the reality is that personal growth doesn't always occur in parallel lines. Sometimes, people grow apart, moving in directions that are not just different but fundamentally incompatible. When values, goals, and worldviews diverge to the point of creating irreconcilable differences, the foundational chemistry, once united, can now cause a negative reaction, disintegrated beyond repair.

Attempts to bridge this divide are often made through couples therapy, self-help books, or even temporary separations. While these can be valuable efforts, there are situations where the emotional and psychological disconnect runs too deep to mend. It's like trying to fit a square peg into a round hole; no matter how much you carve away at the edges, the core shape remains unchanged.

Of course, for children living in such a tense environment, the emotional toll can be significant. They are perceptive and can sense when something is fundamentally amiss between their parents. An unhappy marriage can serve as a profoundly negative example, teaching them that love is fraught with hostility, resentment, or indifference. Do they thrive in this atmosphere? Do they grow up with a healthy understanding of what love and partnership should look like? The answer is a resounding no. The emotional and psychological well-being of the children is compromised, as is that of the parents, trapped in a cycle of unhappiness.

Divorce, despite its daunting nature, can sometimes be the most compassionate course of action. It releases both partners from a dysfunctional dynamic, offering a chance for renewal and growth. The alternative—to remain in a conflicted marriage—often results in greater trauma, intensified by other factors. These external pressures can turn an already painful experience into a traumatic public ordeal, hindering the emotional recovery of all family members.

The path following a divorce can open up avenues for self-discovery and personal growth that might never have been possible within the constraints of a strained marriage. Not only does this benefit the individuals involved, but it also models for the children a courageous act of self-preservation and authentic living. This is not an endorsement to take the idea of divorce lightly but rather an acknowledgment that, in certain circumstances, parting ways can be the healthiest, most ethical, and most loving choice.

It's essential to shed the religious stigmatization of divorce and view it for what it can be—a bold, albeit painful, act of asserting one's boundaries and choosing a path of redemption from an otherwise abusive or toxic reality. By doing so, both partners can embark on separate journeys of self-exploration and growth, potentially leading to healthier relationships. While the experience is undeniably fraught with emotional challenges, the liberation it offers can be the soil in which new, more vital lives can take root. For the sake of everyone involved—especially the children—sometimes divorce is not only justifiable but also the most humane option available.

While divorce may not align with the ultimate will of God, it can sometimes serve as a necessary compromise given the complex and often harsh realities of life. Take the tragic case of my friend Dasha, who lost her life at the hands of an abusive spouse. Suppose her church's religious norms had not hindered her from seeking a divorce. In that case, she might still be alive today, possibly remarried and experiencing love and protection from a new partner. In instances like this, divorce could be not just an option and not only a life-saving escape from a harmful situation- but a way to thrive anew!

Chapter 13

Divorce To Protect Your Family

When it comes to the well-being of a family, especially the children, divorce cannot be discussed lightly. Conventional wisdom may tout the sanctity of the family unit as an untouchable ideal, but we need to consider the quality of life within that unit. Is it not healthier for children to grow up in a peaceful, separated household where they have the opportunity to flourish rather than, for example, in a home permeated by constant abuse, anger, humiliation, emotional detachment, and frequent loud disputes?

Contrary to certain beliefs, divorce can sometimes be advantageous for children's well-being, assuming they still have loving mother and father figures in their lives. It frequently leads to enhanced resilience and communication skills, nurturing a healthier family dynamic. In the process, children absorb crucial lessons in setting boundaries and conflict resolution, which are vital for their emotional and psychological development. Post-divorce, they often form closer, more significant relationships with each parent. The resulting environment tends to be calmer, thereby reducing stress and anxiety. Additionally, divorce bolsters adaptability, empathy, and self-sufficiency in children. In instances of remarriage, they gain the opportunity to observe their parents engaging in healthy relationships and effective communication. This exposure grants children a more grounded and thoughtful understanding of marriage that could otherwise be lacking.

But clinging to a dysfunctional marriage "for the sake of the kids" can, in some cases, do more harm than good. Children are highly perceptive; they pick up on tension, arguments, and the emotional distance between their parents, even when these things are not overtly displayed. The home environment acts as a child's primary context for understanding relationships, emotional management, and conflict resolution. Growing up in a household where discord is the norm rather than the exception can lead to emotional and psychological scars that last a lifetime.

Divorce, in this context, should not be seen as a failure but as an act of self-preservation, an acknowledgment of change, and a commitment to personal growth. As painful as it may be, divorce is an option that can bring about emotional health for both partners and can serve as a significant life lesson for children. Growing up in a house full of tension and bitterness can warp a child's understanding of relationships, love, and emotional well-being. When children see their parents take the difficult but often necessary step of divorce, they can also learn about making tough decisions for the sake of personal happiness and mental health.

Moreover, children in such households are more likely to struggle with issues such as anxiety, depression, low self-esteem, and academic difficulties. The ripple effects can affect their adult lives, influencing their own relationships and even their professional trajectories. On the other hand, when parents make the difficult but sometimes necessary decision to divorce, they model for their children that it's crucial to prioritize well-being and emotional health. Parents can create new, more peaceful homes where children feel secure and loved and have positive role models for relational dynamics by opting for divorce when the marriage is beyond repair.

Additionally, a divorce can sometimes mean that children spend more time with each parent individually. In dysfunctional marriages, it's common for parents to be so consumed by their issues that they don't give their children the attention and emotional support they need. After a divorce, one-on-one time in each household can be more meaningful and beneficial for the child's development.

Of course, divorce is not without its difficulties. It involves change and adaptation, which can be stressful. But isn't it better to undergo a temporary period of adjustment rather than subjecting children to a lifetime imbued with the wrong lessons about love, compromise, and conflict? Importantly, a separated but amicable co-parenting arrangement can provide children with a healthier, more realistic model of adult relationships. It shows them that it is possible to treat each other with respect and kindness, even when things don't work out as initially planned.

While keeping a family together is undoubtedly a noble goal, it should not come at the expense of the emotional well-being and psychological health of its members, especially the children. Otherwise, we once again put the marriage institution in a higher place than the individuals themselves. Unfortunately, in some cases, the most loving, responsible, and courageous act couples can perform for their children is to part ways and forge new paths that offer everyone the peace and happiness they deserve.

Chapter 14

Divorce as a Way to Set Boundaries

T he concept of boundaries, as articulated by Dr. Henry Cloud and Dr. John Townsend in their seminal book "Boundaries" provides a compelling framework for understanding why separation, in some instances, may be the most emotionally and spiritually healthy course of action for all parties involved, including children. At its core, the book emphasizes the crucial role that well-defined boundaries play in cultivating meaningful relationships and protecting individual well-being. These boundaries can manifest in various forms—physical, emotional, or spiritual—and serve as demarcations that help define one's identity, safeguard personal values, and shield against emotional or physical harm.

If we take a cue from Cloud and Townsend and apply it to our subject, a marriage devoid of healthy boundaries is not just flawed but damaging. In a marriage fraught with issues like emotional or physical abuse, continuous neglect, or unresolvable discord, the boundary

that protects one's self-worth, emotional well-being, and even physical safety is frequently violated. This often leads to an erosion of
self-esteem, debilitating emotional states, and a perpetuation of toxic
dynamics that may even pass down to the next generation. In such
instances, initiating a divorce can be seen as the ultimate act of setting
a necessary boundary. It is a way to declare that certain behaviors
and treatments are unacceptable and that the emotional, physical, and
spiritual well-being of the individuals involved—adults and children
alike—must be protected.

Furthermore, the book talks about the "Ten Laws of Boundaries,"
which include taking responsibility for one's boundaries, understanding the impact of one's choices, and respecting the boundaries
of others. In the context of a dysfunctional marriage, divorce is a
way of taking responsibility for enforcing one's boundaries. It's an
acknowledgment that despite best efforts, the marriage has become
a space where healthy limits cannot be maintained. The choice to
divorce, while difficult, shows respect for one's own boundaries and
often engenders mutual respect, as it can free both parties from a cycle
of continuous harm and dysfunction.

One of the significant concerns for many contemplating divorce
is the impact on children. Cloud and Townsend also focus on the
importance of setting boundaries within family dynamics. Children
learn from their environment, and a home filled with strife or emotional detachment sets a harmful example. In contrast, taking the step
to divorce shows children that setting boundaries to protect oneself is
not only acceptable but vital for emotional and psychological health.
It communicates to them that it's okay to prioritize their well-being
over societal norms or expectations, a lesson that will serve them well
in their lives.

The authors address the pitfalls of poor boundary-setting and stress the importance of self-care, self-reflection, and personal growth. A decision to divorce, especially when initiated to end a toxic or destructive marital relationship, can indeed be an act of ultimate self-care. It's a decision that requires substantial self-reflection, courage, and an unwavering commitment to personal growth and emotional well-being for everyone involved.

Conclusions

J udaism's debate around divorce was never centered on the permissibility of divorce itself but rather on the specific circumstances warranting the issuance of a legal document—a bill of divorce. This nuanced discussion shifted in Christianity, morphing into a question of whether divorce is permissible at all. This change can be attributed to the Christian misunderstanding of the original Jewish discourse, partly due to a broader trend of rejecting Jewish practices and teachings, a phenomenon that can be linked to the antisemitism of some of the Church Fathers.

Divorce, according to biblical teachings, isn't inherently sinful. It's a consequence of sin. In cases where trust within a marriage is irreparably damaged, and the relationship can no longer fulfill its divine purpose, divorce becomes a legal and justified resolution. We can try and spiritualize it, but the truth is that sometimes, relationships are so damaged, and patterns or personalities clash in such harmful ways that it is better to separate than to continue suffering. That's why divorce was permitted.

We saw that the biblical narrative provides an example of this when Israel, having broken their covenant, was divorced by God. This action was not only legal but necessary. Marriage is a sacred institution designed to enrich lives, nurture godly offspring, and exemplify the

Creator's principles. However, when a marriage hinders these goals, it may become an idol rather than a means of support.

Why didn't the Bible provide an exhaustive list detailing acceptable grounds for divorce? First, the absence of such details suggests that people are given the freedom to decide when it's time to end a marriage. Second, the Law provided Israel with overarching principles rather than a prescriptive manual for every specific situation. This approach allowed for a degree of interpretative application that could adapt to the nuances of individual cases and cultures. By not delineating every possible scenario, the Law empowered leaders within the community to make informed decisions based on the spirit of the Law—promoting justice, mercy, and faithfulness—rather than merely following a rigid set of rules that might turn irrelevant as society changes. In this way, the Law served as a living document, capable of guiding Israel's leaders through life's moral and ethical complexities (Numbers 11:16-30), including those surrounding the delicate issue of divorce.

Proper hermeneutics require understanding the text as it was perceived by its original audience, not through contemporary Western assumptions. The grounds for divorce, as understood in the context of the time, included issues like cruelty, financial irresponsibility, and neglect of marital duties, paralleling the provisions seen in Exodus 21:10-11. Thus, in biblical terms, divorce is not a sin when it serves as a necessary remedy for a broken relationship, and attempts to fix it were of no avail. In fact, nowhere in the Scriptures is it suggested that divorce is a sin. This idea is merely a conclusion drawn by Western fundamentalists.

When getting divorced means saving your life

When I was actively part of the Messianic movement, the common belief was that leaving a marriage meant weak faith and giving up too easily. Most members thought it showed an unwillingness to work hard or marked you as pitiable and unfit for service. In the eyes of many, divorce was a sign of spiritual weakness, if not outright wickedness. For example, in a large church I used to attend for years, a couple opted for a no-fault divorce. Instead of offering them support during their tough time, the church elders publicly informed all church members of their decision, announcing that the couple was no longer allowed to partake in communion but only attend services as visitors. How humiliating!

Some fundamentalists often forget that relationships can get quite complex and that not everything in life is black and white. Sometimes, things are just too hard to fix, and it's not right to stay in a toxic marriage that makes you anxious, depressed, and unhappy. There are circumstances under which a person might need to exit a marriage, assuming therapy and counseling have proven ineffective, for them to thrive. Some of these can be a significant emotional incompatibility: This is a common issue that can almost never be cured but can only be managed through forceful behavioral modification. For instance, if one partner is emotionally unavailable or abusive in a way they don't even recognize, it can create a severe imbalance. Different people have varying capacities for emotional openness, and this trait is often immutable. When one partner can never meet the emotional needs of the other, it plants the seeds of bitterness, mistrust, and toxicity. And as we know, a relationship cannot survive very long in these conditions.

Another example is a lack of mutual respect or equality. This occurs when one partner believes their desires are more important. It could be a dominant woman or a man demanding blind obedience from his wife, often justifying his demands with selective religious interpretations. For example, I know of a woman who felt compelled to leave her husband because he decided to migrate to another country, and she had no say in the matter.

These are just examples. It's not about being wrong or right; it's about being emotionally healthy, thriving, and happy.

An appeal to pastors and spiritual leaders

As we reach the conclusion of this book, it's vital to address the complexities and responsibilities inherent in spiritual leadership, particularly those of church pastors.

First and foremost, the believer must understand that pastors are not arbiters of marital fate. A pastor or minister has the authority to officiate marriages, but they do not have any authority to divorce couples. The pastor's role is to support and relieve the couple and family in their time of stress, not vice versa. Whether to stay married or divorce is a highly personal decision. It is not the pastor's role to approve or disapprove of divorces. While a pastor's spiritual counsel may be sought, their guidance should never replace the expertise of certified psychologists or marriage counselors, especially because pastors often lack formal training in these disciplines and may be biased by their own religious views.

The intersection of faith and human psychology is a delicate space to navigate. Unfortunately, many pastors opt to wield their influence not through a balanced and educated view but by misusing or taking scriptural verses out of context. It's easy to quote the Bible to justify virtually any perspective, but interpreting it in a way that benefits the psychological and spiritual health of a person is where the real challenge lies. Some pastors, alas, employ these texts recklessly, playing Russian roulette with people's lives and mental health- and on top of it, they do so in the name of God! If they believe that "God hates divorce," I would like to remind them that God despises the misuse of His name by spiritual authorities to advance their own views or agendas:

> "You shall not misuse the name of the Lord your God,
> for the Lord will not hold anyone guiltless who mis-
> uses his name." (Exodus 20:7)

I know this through personal experience. When my wife and I went through the process of divorce, my own pastors made sweeping claims about the irrelevance of our personal happiness to God, drawing on a superficial reading of divine will. One of them also used spiritual manipulation and fear tactics, peddling stories about how God punished their friend's decision to divorce through terminal cancer. Such perspectives don't just distort God's character; they also inflict emotional and psychological harm on those who are already suffering.[1] Spiritual leaders may be likable, friendly, and amiable, yet when their influence and beliefs are rooted in uneducated views, they often become a recipe for significant harm.

While faith plays a significant role in our lives, it's important to remember that everyone has a need for a private space, a sanctuary for personal struggles that may not necessarily be open for pastoral intervention. In instances where pastors are involved in multiple dimensions of community life, their influence can become overwhelming and intrusive if not properly bounded. These spiritual leaders might feel entitled to weigh in on issues that are better left to certified professionals, creating a level of exposure that can be uncomfortable and, in many cases, inappropriate and damaging (James 3:1).

These elders, often familiar with only a fraction of someone's life circumstances, tend to judge harshly based on their limited perspective. They either were unaware or chose to overlook the fact that they were missing the broader context of the situation. Such harsh scrutiny is not only unfair but can also be damaging. It erodes trust and fosters an environment where people hesitate to be open about their real-life challenges.

Male pastors, particularly in conservative fundamentalist churches, often lack an understanding of the experiences of women and wives within their congregations. They may not fully comprehend the fear and humiliation a woman can face when subjected to abuse by a man, or the terror of fearing for her own life. As shepherds of their flock, their primary responsibility should be "safety first." This aligns with the Biblical principle found in 1 Corinthians 7:15, where God expresses a desire for His people to live in peace.

If you are a Christian pastor, your role is monumental. A shepherd is not a psychologist, a legal mediator, or a judge. Pastors are shepherds, the protectors of their flock. Take this responsibility to heart. Jesus asked Peter in John 21:17: *"Do you love me? Feed my sheep."* If you love your community, guide them towards pastures of peace, growth, and well-being. Help and teach your flock to defend themselves, their rights, and their family members. Use your position not to dominate and control but to serve, not to intimidate but to inspire, and not to harm but to heal. A shepherd's primary duty is to ensure the safety and welfare of the flock, not to control their lives by making their decisions for them. That line differentiates between a supportive and healthy Christian community and a cult. Remember, you are tasked with tending to fragile souls and must handle them with the utmost care.

A word for those in abusive or toxic relationships:

Know that your well-being is essential to God, who loves you and wants the best for you! Do not endure suffering in silence, thinking it's a cross you're divinely ordained to bear. There are professionals trained to help you navigate these complex emotional and psychological landscapes, and you owe it to yourself to seek them out. Faith is crucial, but it should not replace professional help or, in cases when needed, legal guidance. I encourage those in distress in their marriage to seek professional help, make their own decisions, and, if needed and left without a choice, take the necessary steps toward their well-being and happiness—even if they fear no one else will understand.

A concluding message to those who have gone through a divorce, particularly men:

Regardless of the difficulties in your divorce, it's crucial to continue supporting your ex-partner, especially when children are involved. Often, the wife may have dedicated many years to raising the family and supporting your career, possibly at the expense of her own professional development. Now, your partner might face the challenge of rebuilding her life without a career foundation. Despite any bitterness that may have accompanied the divorce, extending grace and ensuring your former spouse's and children's well-being is essential.

***

Before you close this book (or turn off your e-reader), I have a favor to ask. I've dedicated significant effort to creating this book and would deeply appreciate it if you could spare a few seconds to rate it on Amazon. Leaving a review would mean the world to me! I make it a point to read every review. A great deal of time went into researching and distilling this topic into a concise, easily digestible read for you. Rating or reviewing my book is a wonderful way for you to return the favor.

Thank you so much for your attention and consideration.

Dr. Eitan Bar

P.S. I have written several other books on various spiritual topics. You are welcome to check them out!

---

1. You might say, and rightly so, that the Messianic movement, where I've spent the last twenty years, tends to be on the rigid, harsh, and legalistic side. While that may be true in many instances, I also personally know many people outside the Messianic movement who have gone through a divorce and have suffered severely at the hands of pastors and other Christians.

Printed in Great Britain
by Amazon